THE ROBBIE WILLIAMS STORY

UNAUTHORISED & UNOFFICIAL

EMMA MORGAN

THIS IS A SEVENOAKS BOOK

FIRST PUBLISHED BY IN GREAT BRITAIN
BY SEVENOAKS IN 2004
20 MORTIMER STREET
LONDON W1T 3JW

TEXT AND DESIGN COPYRIGHT ©
CARLTON BOOKS LTD 2004

ISBN 1 86200 190 1

PRINTED AND BOUND IN DUBAI

10 9 8 7 6 5 4 3 2 1

WORDS: EMMA MORGAN
EDITED BY: AUBERGINE
ART DIRECTOR: DAVID HICKS
PHOTOS: REX FEATURES

THE ROBBIE WILLIAMS STORY

UNAUTHORISED & UNOFFICIAL

EMMA MORGAN

SevenOaks

CONTENTS

chapter 1

LET ME ENTERTAIN YOU

O N 13 FEBRUARY 1974 GLAM ROCKERS MUD WERE AT NUMBER ONE in the UK with their ludicrous love song *Tiger Feet*, wholesome brother-and-sister duo The Carpenters' *The Singles 1969-1973* was at the top of the album charts, and Peter and Teresa Jeanette (Jan) Williams were welcoming their son, Robert Peter, into the world. Joining the party in North Staffs Maternity Hospital, Newcastle-under-Lyme, were Pete's mum, Betty ("Nan"), and baby Robert's ten-year-old half-sister, Sally (from Jan's first marriage), both of whom would soon dote on the newborn.

The Williams clan had more to celebrate that year when stand-up comedian Pete appeared in the finals of TV talent show *New Faces*, under the stage name he still uses to this day: Pete Conway. (He came third; Les Dennis was second and finalist Victoria Wood wasn't even placed.) The newborn Robert might have been too young to appreciate his Dad's success but he had certainly acquired Pete's performing gene.

Taking a break from The Red Lion, the pub they ran and lived above in Burslem, Stoke-on-Trent (down the road from the grounds of Port Vale Football Club), Jan and Sally took toddler Robert to the Spanish resort of Torremolinos in the summer of 1978. As Punk Rock exploded back home, Robert's mindset was stuck firmly in the 1950s.

When Jan's back was turned at a local talent show ("She was actually shitting herself because she couldn't find me"), he ran off and added himself to the bill. Announced as "Robert from England", the four-year-old used his time in the spotlight to impersonate John Travolta, having taught himself *Summer Nights* by repeatedly listening to the *Grease* soundtrack on the pub jukebox. He won.

Performing, Robert soon learned, brought rewards of adoration – "Literally before I could talk, I could sing and I found if I did that people smiled and paid me attention" – and offered a release from the pain of his father's sudden absence.

Having travelled down to Wembley to watch Manchester United play Liverpool in the 1977 FA Cup final (which United won, 2–1), Pete made up his mind on the terraces to leave Jan. He didn't come home again except, some time later, to ask for his clothes. Years of long-distance summer seasons and residencies at clubs around the country had taken their toll on the marriage; running a pub with his wife had been an opportunity for Pete to spend more time with the family, but it proved a disaster.

The person who had most encouraged Robert's exhibitionism and talents – often allowing the pre-schooler to entertain regulars during late-night lock-ins (much to Jan's annoyance), when he'd stand at the top of the stairs bathed in the landing light, singing, dancing and doing impressions of Frank Spencer and football coach Brian Clough – became no more than a weekends-and-holidays Dad. Saturdays now consisted of Robert playing football with "this bloke who used to come round, take me off to *Woolies* and buy me a toy car" in the park, then placing bets at the bookies and watching the results together on *Grandstand* (he grew to hate the routine). Holidays were spent at camps and

CHAPTER OPENER: THE CHEEKY CHAPPIE WAS A PERSONA ROB ADOPTED EARLY ON

RIGHT: SCHOOL CHUMS CONSIDERED HIM THE CLASS CLOWN

caravan parks where Pete had summer season bookings, watching – and learning from – the evening entertainment.

After The Red Lion, Jan ran a series of businesses – a boutique, a coffee shop and a florist – while raising Robert single-handedly, but still found the time to treat her son. In 1981, she took him to his first concert, 50s rock'n'roll revivalists Showaddywaddy at the Queen's Hall in Burslem, around the corner from their old pub. It had a lasting effect on the seven-year-old: "I wanted the Teddy Boy outfit and everything but me mum wouldn't get me one because she thought I'd grow out of it."

The following year, Robert and Jan stayed in the Victoria Falls Hotel in Zimbabwe. Spotting an important-looking local in the lobby surrounded by armed guards, he strolled up to him and declared, "Hello, I'm Robert from England and I can do impressions of black men", before imitating 1975 *New Faces* winner Lenny Henry. Joshua Nkomo, the black activist and future vice-president of Zimbabwe, just laughed and signed an autograph. "He was fascinated that a kid could just come up to him when he had these men with machine guns, a kid who wasn't scared," Robbie later recalled.

Jan continued to support her son's interests as Pete had done, encouraging him to join performance societies and take part in school shows. While attending Mill Hill Primary School, Robert was regarded as "plump and short... a bit big-headed and pushy" but he shone when cast in productions, most notably as Fagin, the surrogate father of a group of young thieves in *Oliver!*.

Outside of school, Robert joined the North Staffordshire Amateur Operatic and Dramatic Society (Jan joined too, for moral support) and the Stoke-on-Trent Charity Pantomime and Drama Company, amongst other am-dram groups, as well as taking extra-curricular lessons in dance. (His academic success began to suffer as a result; undiagnosed dyslexia was also to blame.) A North Staffs production of *Hans Christian Anderson*, the musical version of the storyteller's life, was to be Robert's first professional public appearance. At the age of nine, he was seen in a chorus of children singing and dancing while enjoying the fairytales.

Two years later he won his first lead, as Jeremy, the son of flying-car inventor Caractacus Potts, in *Chitty Chitty Bang Bang* after answering an advert Jan spotted in their local paper, *The Sentinel*. Auditioning alongside 30 other boys, Robert won the role with a rendition of the show's song, *Truly Scrumptious*, and despite his dyslexia he went on to learn every word of the script, not just his own part. More local productions followed and Jan proudly cut out and kept all mentions of her prodigious son in the local newspapers.

In September 1985 Robert started at St Margaret Ward Roman Catholic High School, two days late due to his commitments with *Chitty Chitty Bang Bang*. With no provision for drama or musical productions, the school offered Rob – as he now preferred to be known – few outlets for his performance skills. He began to lead a double life, combining an increasingly-confident stage persona out-of-school with his real, insecure self at school – for starters, he kept his musical success a secret from new-found friends, pretending his delayed enrolment was due to a holiday.

Still a little overweight, Rob deflected taunts of "Fatsykins" from fellow pupils with the humour he inherited from his father; in time, they thought of him as the class clown, "a brilliant laugh [and] full of energy". As his popularity grew, so did his interest in the opposite sex. He bombarded older potential girlfriends with gifts of chocolates, flowers and tapes of their favourite bands, but his ability to make them laugh was his biggest draw. He sometimes succeeded in going on dates with the objects of his desire but they would prove to be short-lived affairs, usually resulting in little more than "a quick peck in the playground". And girls lost their allure when the prospect of being "one of the lads" arose.

Amused by his impressions of Sylvester Stallone's Rambo on the way home from school – which involved pulling his tie up around his head and jumping over hedges – the lads' gang in his year eventually allowed Rob, or "Willwogs" (and occasionally, "Swellhead") as they nicknamed him, into their confidence. He became firm friends with Giuseppe Romano (known to the gang as "Gius"), Peter O'Reilly ("PO 2") and Philip Lindsay ("Lino"), but he was closest to Lee Hancock ("Tate"). They bonded over a shared love of "The rudest, crudest, lewdest, drunkest band in Christendom", The Macc Lads (responsible for an obscene spoof of Tina Turner's *Nutbush City Limits* entitled *Knutsford Scabby Women*), and cult Channel 4 comedy *Vic Reeves' Big Night Out*. "We talked about Vic Reeves, Macc Lads, beer and football," recalled Lee. "We never worried about exams. It didn't matter and we didn't care."

Rob's humour and charisma might have won over his schoolfriends, but teachers at St Margaret Ward would be another matter. His poor results, silly behaviour in lessons and occasional truancy failed to endear him to the staff, and several members would inspire the poem *Hello Sir*, hidden at the end of his first solo album, *Life Thru A Lens*. "Hello Sir, remember me?/I'm the man you thought I'd never be/The boy who you reduced to tears/The lad called 'Thingy' for six whole years... Well, I'm here, and you're still there/With your fake sports car and receding hair... As for now I've a different weapon/Stage and screen is about to beckon."

In 1988, North Staffs were preparing a production of *Oliver!*. This time, the role he wanted was that of charming pickpocket The Artful Dodger, arguably a better part than the angelic orphan Oliver Twist. He turned up to audition at the Queen's Theatre alongside 150 other boys and, with a rendition of The Artful Dodger's signature song, *Consider Yourself* won the part.

"The first night I walked out from the side of the stage," recalled Rob, "whistling and doing this walk, the whole audience just gasped. I physically heard them do it. I'd just won them over by walking on to the stage. They hadn't seen anything I could do yet."

Rob's mood was soon overwhelmed by the arrival of an unexpected guest. As he walked offstage after his first scene, he cried. He told a friend that he'd spotted his dad, Pete – who was supposed to be midway through a summer season – sitting in the front row: "How I remembered any of the words I don't know..." (Pete's reaction to his son's starring role, during which he improvised some juggling with prop oranges from a market stall, was a proud – if muttered – "Flash git".)

He soon composed himself and went back onstage and finished the show. "I can always remember coming out for the curtain call and my cheers drowning everybody else's," he said later. "I thought, I really am good at this."

After the applause died down, disappointment awaited the euphoric Rob at the after-show party. A glamorous-looking Jan, clad in a fur coat, was waiting with her "smarmy" new boyfriend and a brown paper bag she handed to Rob. It contained his pyjamas, and the message was clear to him. "I'll have to sort something out for tonight," he told another actor, meaning he wasn't to come home that night.

As a career in showbusiness was becoming ever more likely for Rob, he was also developing a fondness for drink and drugs. Rob got drunk for the first time at the age of 13, when visiting Pete at a holiday camp in Scarborough. While watching his dad's routine he persuaded the barman to let him have free bottles of Newcastle Brown Ale, which he guzzled despite hating the taste. The second time, at home some months later, he managed to smash a framed picture of his hero Muhammad Ali (in wealthier times, he replaced it with an expensive Andy Warhol screen-printed version). These weren't isolated incidents for long – as the lads grew older, they regularly drank and smoked, as well as experimenting with sniffing aerosols and sharing joints. Rob even claimed to have been under the influence of alcohol and LSD when he took his GCSEs.

Although his allegiances were now to his mates, who "would have a laugh at the girls' expense", the 15-year-old Rob found himself powerless to refuse the advances of a newcomer to St Margaret Ward, Liverpudlian Ann Marie Lawson. She soon singled out Rob and told him in no uncertain terms – in front of the lads – that she was going to "shag" him: "Your place, Friday after school." Rob went through with her challenge, if only to avoid being mocked by his mates. "I took her up to my room and about two-and-a-half minutes later it was all over," Rob recalled later. "It was a less than impressive performance, but I was thrilled and naturally told all my mates what a stud I'd been."

As a child, Robert had shown little interest in pop stars – his singing heroes were the crooners his dad loved, demonstrated by his rendition of Ella Fitzgerald's *Ev'ry Time We Say Goodbye* at the post-exams school disco – preferring to idolise sportsmen. The proximity of Port Vale FC to his childhood home had inevitably made him a huge fan and his bedroom walls were covered with football pictures (in one, "The whole Oxford United team had one bollock hanging out, that was my favourite"). In addition to playing football well he was also an accomplished golfer, elected Burslem Golf Club's junior captain at the age of 15.

Nevertheless, when Jan saw another advert in *The Sentinel*, for the fifth member of a new, Manchester-based boy band, Rob decided to give it a go. At the audition in Manchester he was asked to sing Aussie star Jason Donovan's debut solo single *Nothing Can Divide Us* with the other four members of the band – who had already been recruited. The band's soon-to-be manager Nigel Martin-Smith was certainly impressed: "There was just this glint in his eye as he looked at me and I thought, 'You've got to be in the band'."

With little else to occupy him, Rob spent what remained of the summer holidays binge drinking with Lee, not least when he found out his GCSE results – he'd failed them all. Dejected and drunk, he made his way home to tell his mum. But before he could get the words out, Jan told him the news that would change his life: "You're in that band." Rob ran up to his room, threw open the window and bellowed, "I'm going to be famous!".

chapter 2

COULD IT BE
MAGIC?

AFTER ROB'S EUPHORIA FADED, THE WILLIAMS FAMILY DEBATED the wisdom of letting a 16-year-old sign up for life in the entertainment industry. When his adoring Nan gave her approval – "I'd be more worried if he was going to become a priest" – the fateful decision was made. With Rob still a minor, Jan acted as signatory on his contract in September 1990 and would continue to keep a close watch on her son's earnings. At the audition Nigel recalled, "She fired 20 questions at me and gave me the hardest time."

The audition had also been Rob's introduction to the people who would be his bandmates for the foreseeable future; his first impression of frontman elect Gary Barlow was not good. Describing him as "a guy with spiky hair looking really fucking dated in these horrible tracksuit bottoms and shitty trainers [with] a briefcase and music score sheets," Rob recalled his first words being, "I write the songs because I'm Gary Barlow."

Like Rob, 19-year-old Gary had his childhood interest in performing nurtured by his parents. At the age of 10 he was offered a choice of Christmas presents; between a BMX bike and a keyboard, he chose the latter. (The young Elvis Presley's future was determined in a similar way – he asked for a bike for his 11th birthday but, fearing for his safety, his overprotective parents bought him a guitar instead.) He was soon able to copy tunes he heard, note-perfect, on "this bloody organ" and became intent upon emulating the success of singer-songwriter superstars George Michael and Elton John. He established himself on the north west's working men's club circuit and entered talent shows, making the semi-finals of a BBC TV songwriting contest entitled "A Song For Christmas". Footage still exists of the pink-cheeked Gary singing *Let's Pray For Christmas*, clad in a woolly jumper and scarf for effect, and although he didn't win he was given a prize of studio time that he put to good use. Gary circulated demo tapes of his original compositions – including future hit *A Million Love Songs* – around the music industry, but only one person overlooked his physical failings (he was stocky and decidedly unhip, with a slight squint) and recognised the potential of his songwriting.

Inspired by the global success (and rudeness) of the Bostonian boy band New Kids On The Block, Mancunian entrepreneur Nigel had come up with the idea of putting together a well-mannered British version. Prepared to put a substantial amount of his own money into the venture, Nigel realised that young composer Gary's talents could form the core of his dream group and persuaded him he was too young to make it solo.

Gary brought 18-year-old Mark Owen to Nigel's attention – the two teenagers had met at a local recording studio and formed a duo, The Cutest Rush, in which they both sang original Barlow songs and classic cover versions. Mark's good looks added sex appeal to the embryonic band's assets.

Nigel had already been approached by 20-year-old Jason Orange and 22-year-old

Howard Donald, who were seeking management for their dance duo, Street Machine. They too had a history of entering talent competitions and Nigel realised their muscle-bound moves could give the band a kinetic, eye-catching quality beyond Mark's shy smiles, that would detract from the fact that Gary was – by his own frank admission – "crap at dancing".

With choreography, singing, songwriting and eye-candy taken care of, recruiting a fifth member was largely a means of lightening the promotional load ahead, Nigel's insurance policy against any of the other four dropping out. Perhaps because his role within the band was undefined, latecomer Rob felt like an outsider from the very beginning. "I definitely felt manipulated from the off," he said later, "...and from day one I felt I was being deliberately ostracised."

As at school, Rob used his humour to make the best of a bad situation – although no longer fat he was instructed to lose more weight, and as the youngest member by almost two years he was often blamed when things went wrong – and soon carved out a niche within the band as "the funny one". "I thought my manager hated me, and that he told the boys he hated me," Rob recalled. "I thought the boys treated me like an idiot, and that I was always a scapegoat for everybody else's misfortunes, so it's like, when you feel like an idiot, you act like one. My mechanism against it was to joke."

So bad did Rob feel about his "whipping boy" status in the band, he almost left before they'd recorded a single note. He told his parents he'd rather be a Blue Coat at a holiday camp, but Pete talked him into staying: "Can you imagine seeing them on television while you live in a caravan, ironing your own shirts [and] buying your own toilet rolls?"

His insecurity wasn't helped by Nigel's insistence that he change his name from Rob to the more boy band-sounding "Robbie", which he hated. (He also acquired a new middle name, "Maximillian", for publicity purposes, if only because it rhymed with Williams.) The band, which until now had the working name of Kick It, was rechristened too. A photo caption on a picture of Madonna in a tabloid reading 'Take that and party!' was soon adopted instead. An anthemic song was duly penned by Gary with the same title, but ultimately the group became known as simply Take That.

During the six long months of rehearsals that followed, Nigel outlined his strategy for the band. In a move that has since become *de rigeur* for all new pop acts, he intended to promote them directly to the gay market and the relatively recession-proof "pink pound". Gay himself, Nigel knew the scene and was aware that personal appearances from male acts – as opposed to aging disco divas – were enough of a rarity for Take That to become infamous fast. All five were kitted out in homoerotic lycra and leather costumes; in a TV interview, "Robbie" described their look as "Bad boys made good".

Nigel also appointed himself the secret sixth member of the band, telling the others: "If we stick together, form a wall around ourselves and keep away from parties, the tabloid press will have nothing to knock us with when we achieve fame." To this end, he instigated a series of basic rules to prevent anyone jeopardising their future success: No Smoking, No Drinking, No Girls, No Drugs. To Mark, Gary, Jason and Howard, the rules were Draconian but easy enough to bend when "urges" arose – aged 18 and above, they'd got most of their youthful rebellion out of the way already. (Howard said recently, "Nigel Martin-Smith obviously thought that we [weren't] sleeping with girls in the early days, but he didn't know anything.") For Rob, it was the denial of yet another part of his 16-year-old's lifestyle – he was apparently overweight, his own name was no good, and now he wasn't even allowed to enjoy himself.

The band's live debut came in Flicks nightclub in Huddersfield, West Yorkshire. They earned themselves £20 for gyrating in front of less than 50 people to some of Gary's Hi-NRG compositions. A seemingly endless tour of gay nights around the country followed. Confident the band were fulfilling his vision, Nigel began to tout them to record companies. A&R man and *Pop Idol* judge Simon Cowell was unimpressed by their early demo and press shots and passed on the chance to sign them. "I didn't think the songs were very good... and I didn't like the fact that the band seemed to be centred around Gary Barlow – I just didn't think he looked like a front man."

Undaunted, Nigel decided to bypass the record companies and put out their first single himself, on a label he named Dance UK. *Do What You Like*, released in July 1991, was an unremarkable pumping, 80s-sounding dance track with Italian house-style synthesiser, and were it not for the accompanying video – self-financed by Nigel at £5,000 – it might have been the last anyone heard of Take That.

By now, Nigel had decided on a two-pronged attack. As well as courting the pink pound, the pre-famous five were targeting pocket money too, with schools tours. For around two years, the band would play three or more sets a day, at schools in the morning, under-18s venues in the early evening and nightclubs towards midnight. Because of this, their first video had to appeal to both audiences. The pre-watershed version featured the five semi-naked and throwing jelly at each other; the post-watershed edit had them completely naked, lying in a line with their rears facing the camera. If nothing else, it made the teen magazines finally take notice of this outrageous – if still unsigned – band, and they begAn to appear in their pages. Simon Cowell had by now noticed the sudden groundswell of support for the act and called Nigel to re-open negotiations. He was too late – after almost a year of exhausting self-improvement and promotion, during which *Do What You Like* reached only Number 82 in the charts, Take That signed to RCA in September 1991. If anything, it only increased the pressure on the band.

The multiple daily PAs continued, but press commitments were now added to their burden. When their first two RCA singles flopped – *Promises* made it into the Top 40, just, at Number 38, but the follow-up, *Once You've Tasted Love*, fell short, at Number 45 – it looked like they might be dropped from the label. For their third – and perhaps final – RCA single, *It Only Takes A Minute*, the band's image was radically revamped and their appeal tailored specifically to their pubescent female fans. Lyrically, too, there was no longer any ambiguity about the band's sexuality: "It only takes a minute, girl/To fall in love". The re-style paid off, and Take That achieved their first Top 10 hit – *It Only Takes A Minute* peaked at Number Seven.

For the next single, producer Ian Levine suggested to Gary that Rob should be allowed to sing lead vocals. "His face dropped, and the colour drained out of his

cheeks and he says 'Why? ... [I'm] the lead singer'," recalled Ian. "He was almost in tears." As *I Found Heaven* wasn't a Barlow original, written instead by Ian and backing singer Billy Griffin, he got his way, and Rob's first lead vocal made it to Number 15 in August 1992. While Gary would sing lead on 11 of the 13 tracks on debut album *Take That And Party*, released in September 1992 and peaking at Number Two, Rob was permitted one more outing. *Could It Be Magic* was released in December the same year and gave the band their biggest hit yet, reaching Number Three. Although Levine recorded it, the single was remixed by The Rapino Brothers for release and he was shocked when he heard it. "They kept Robbie's lead vocal [but] on the chorus ... they'd sampled Billy Griffin's vocal part and kept repeating it, and left all the Take That vocals out!" The single would bag the band their first Brit Award at the following year's ceremony, yet only Rob appeared on it – in essence, he achieved his first solo Brit six years before anyone realised.

As Take That's profile grew the 'cheeky chappie' persona of Robbie became almost equal in popularity to Mark's doe-eyed sex symbol with their fans, but Rob's standing within the group hadn't improved. While he and Mark had formed a strong friendship – the youngest two, they also bonded over football, Mark having had trials for Huddersfield Town, Rochdale and Manchester United before acquiring a groin injury – he still felt like the runt of the litter. As tours took him ever further away from the reassuring influence of his family, he sought an outlet for his angst-ridden feelings of unworthiness. "We were in Düsseldorf, in the middle of a European tour... and I was really sad. About everything that was going on around me, the position I'd put myself in," recalled Rob. "So I started writing poetry to release some of it. I just thought, I am worthwhile, I have a talent."

He'd previously contributed an uncredited, heavily-distorted rap to the end of *Once You've Tasted Love* – "Come into my world as the badness disappears/Take my hand, don't be afraid, I'm gonna work out all your fears..." – but lyrics were another matter entirely. Having written a song inspired by prostitutes in Manchester, Rob sang it down the phone to Gary. "It's alright that, lad," he replied, adding to someone out of Rob's earshot, "That Robbie's started writing stuff. It would be alright if we were a rock'n'roll band." For now, Rob's poetry would stay private and original Take That material would be credited to 'G Barlow'.

Why Can't I Wake Up With You? would be the band's eighth single in February 1993, and fans' first taster of their second album *Everything Changes* – it reached Number Two, kept off the top spot by Shaggy's dancehall smash *Oh Carolina*. It would be the first of six singles from the album, four of which – *Pray*, *Relight My Fire* (in the video for which Mark wore a prophetic 'Junkie's Baddy Powder' t-shirt), *Babe* and *Everything Changes* (with a lead vocal from Robbie) – finally gave them the Number Ones they'd been craving since 1990. On the sleeve, Robbie's dedication read, "Three years on and still rockin'. As the title says, 'Everything Changes' (but you) and that's so, so true. All my love. Up the Vale... Robbie." (Port Vale FC estimated his support was bringing them £1,000 a week in replica team shirt sales at the time.)

Sold-out arena tours around the world replaced the club PAs forever – Simon Cowell

PREVIOUS PAGE:
ROB AND HIS
BAND-MATES AT THE
BRIT AWARDS IN
1993 – HE WOULD
GO ON TO WIN MORE
BRITS THAN ANY
OTHER PERFORMER

admits, "To this day, I've never seen better pop shows" — but their hard-won success was becoming a burden. While Nigel had set up an official Take That fan club and given Rob's sister Sally a job working for it — at its height, it had over 70,000 members — Jan's florist, "Bloomers", was forced to close due to the volume of visits from Robbie fans. After the whereabouts of the family home became known (as well as countless ex-directory phone numbers), Jan was forced to put it on the market, for £57,950. Rob's Nan was more welcoming to the fans who sought out her home, sometimes even inviting them in for tea, and couldn't care less if Nigel disapproved. "I will do what I want; he's my grandson and I'm proud of him."

Far too busy to look into his own finances — and increasingly more distracted by drugs, having taken cocaine for the first time before a recent arena show — Rob asked Jan to check that everything was above board while he was out of the country. "There were a lot of things happening with the accounts and Nigel Martin-Smith and Take That which I didn't understand, so I got my mother to interview the accountant," he said. "In my view, if there's not a problem, then my mother should be let in to see for herself." Earning a wage of only £150 a week from an act that would soon have sold over 10 million singles and nine million albums, not counting the millions merchandising would have brought them, Rob felt he had every right to be curious. Nigel disagreed.

While the group were touring Australia in the summer of 1994, Nigel faxed the rest of the band a cease-and-desist letter he'd sent Jan in response to her perceived snooping. "Such a vile letter, condemning my mother and making me out as the black sheep of the band," recalled Rob. "Nigel Martin-Smith was scared of my mother, but he succeeded in turning the rest of the band against her." Rob documented his outrage in the poem that became *No Regrets*: "I know from the outside/We looked good for each other/Felt things were going wrong/When you didn't like my mother."

A third album, *Nobody Else*, was swiftly written and slickly produced with the lucrative American market in mind. With the exception of another rap, credited to "Sure" — "Holdin', squeezin', touchin', teasin'/Wantin', wishin', waitin', thinkin'... Blindin', groovin', feel it movin'/Findin', breathin', bracin', breedin'/With you, girl" — Rob's contribution to the record was negligible. With both Howard and Mark sharing lead vocals with Gary, Robbie's absence was glaring but entirely self-inflicted: "I abused my voice and I paid the price." After years of appearing to accept Nigel's rules (and being berated in weekly "Behaviour Meetings" by the rest of the band, too) Rob had slowly broken them all. "He wanted to lead his life the way he believed a star should enjoy himself," said Nigel. "For Robbie it became all about the party." For once, Rob agreed with his manager, saying "If I hadn't taken drugs and slept with girls when I was in a pop group I would have been abnormal." Even Gary would later admit "I've done cocaine, ecstasy and smoked dope... I slept with hundreds of fans all over the world."

Aside from embracing outlawed substances, Rob began to alter his physical appearance, dying his hair bright blue without consent and acquiring his first tattoo, an ornate Maltese cross on his right hip. Having previously taken care to never be photographed with cigarettes, he was now snapped smoking and stumbling drunkenly out of nightclubs; that summer he experienced his first Glastonbury Festival. With

rock'n'roll newcomers Oasis on the second stage, Rob quietly joined the crowd — only *Smash Hits* spotted his distinctive features amongst a sea of brunette heads — but he spent most of his time backstage, drinking privately with former Undertones singer Feargal Sharkey on dance act M People's coach.

Nigel was desperate that Robbie shouldn't disrupt the band's momentum, especially as he was preparing to take the band to America, which would take everyone's full concentration. But short of forcing him into rehab — which he daren't do, in case the news filtered through to the tabloids — he was powerless to prevent his excess.

On 24 November 1994, Take That appeared at the inaugural MTV Europe Music Awards in Berlin to perform new single *Sure* and collect the gong for Best Group. To insider Alex Kadis, a former *Smash Hits* writer and then the official Take That biographer, it was apparent that Robbie was in a bad way, even during the ceremony: "I remember... looking at Robbie and thinking, 'He looks like a dead man walking'."

It was at a private party in the hotel later that things got seriously out of control; Naomi Campbell's former PA Rebecca White recalled "There was a lot of cocaine." Woken in the middle of the night to take care of her employer, she remembered "Robbie's manager came running into the suite... and Robbie was carried out of the room." Alex was later told by both Nigel and Rob himself that "Robbie had been going up and down in the lift for a few minutes with black vomit all over himself... and it still didn't get in the papers." Had the tabloids caught on, Robbie's immediate future would have been different, but as long as Nigel still had some control over the public image of the band he had a stay of execution.

In May 1995, *Nobody Else* was finally released. With a *Sgt. Pepper's Lonely Hearts Club Band*-style cover collage of sweets and memorabilia, the inner sleeve featured moody shots of the band looking old and exhausted (despite new hairstyles courtesy of Vidal Sassoon). A more mature-sounding album than the previous two, it was lyrically obsessed with relationships and break-ups and forthcoming single *Never Forget* could have been written with the demise of the band in mind: "Never forget where you've come here from/Never pretend that it's all real/Someday soon this will be someone else's dream..." The album went straight to Number One, as lead single *Sure* and the band's career-defining follow-up *Back For Good* had already done.

The same month, Take That were invited back to MTV for the top-rated show *Most Wanted*. Wearing a T-shirt emblazoned with the words 'MY BOOZE HELL', Rob debuted a freshly-bleached shock of hair. When asked by host Ray Cokes if the band would ever pose naked, Robbie said he'd do it for "a tenner". A girl in the audience immediately produced a £10 note, which Mark responded to by saying he would actually only do it for 10 *old* pounds (the notes had recently changed). "No, I'd do it for new pounds," said Robbie. "As long as it's £10 I don't care." With that, he dropped his trousers and "mooned" an estimated audience of 60 million viewers across Europe.

Nigel's private problems with Robbie had just become very public; it seemed his youngest charge had learnt little from his near-death experience in Berlin and was intent upon sabotaging what remained of his and Take That's squeaky-clean image and career. The worst was yet to come.

(BLEACHED) BLONDS HAVE MORE FUN: ROB'S COCAINE-SNORTING, BOOZING ANTICS SEEMED A DELIBERATE PLOY TO SABOTAGE WHAT WAS LEFT OF HIS, AND TAKE THAT'S SQUEAKY-CLEAN IMAGE

chapter 3

no
REGRETS

THE MORE OF HIS REAL SELF ROB CHOSE TO EXPOSE TO THE PUBLIC, THE MORE HE questioned his confinement within Take That. "'Why can't I go out there, why can't I do that?' I'd ask myself," he recalled. "So one day I went, 'I've had enough,' went and did it. That's when I discovered why I couldn't."

The 1995 Glastonbury Festival was approaching and Rob asked Nigel's permission to attend. Perhaps in the hope of placating and taming him the manager said yes, but only on the grounds that he would take a minder with him for the weekend. Rob decided instead to help himself to 16 bottles of champagne from an RCA party and, having stashed them in the boot of a Jaguar with blacked-out windows, was driven towards the site in Somerset, sampling the drink en route. He arrived at the backstage enclosure on Friday 23 June in style, if far from sober and, through a mutual acquaintance of Noel Gallagher's future wife Meg Mathews, gained an audience with Oasis. Liam Gallagher's first words upon seeing the inebriated blonde pop star were, "Take fuckin' what?"

Rob was thereafter inseparable from the Manchester band, even during their set that night. Tim Abbott of Oasis' label Creation Records was on hand with a camcorder throughout much of the festival; his footage shows Rob once again acting the fool in order to be accepted, both off-stage and on. Three songs into Oasis' headline show, Liam shouted "Come on!" to Rob, who was watching in the wings of the Pyramid stage. He lumbered into view during *Shakermaker* and delivered 30 seconds' shambling dancing before trudging off again and singing along (although further footage shows he didn't actually know the words, or was perhaps so drunk he'd forgotten them).

Having by now acquired a blacked-out front tooth courtesy of some gaffer tape, Rob gave interviews to anyone who approached him backstage, another violation of Nigel's strictly-controlled PR campaign. While appearances indicated that Rob had little control over his actions that weekend, he later claimed it was all part of his masterplan to escape Take That. "I was at Glastonbury for a reason. Primarily, I was there for effect, and also to meet the Oasis lads. I hadn't been allowed to do interviews or photos without someone from the record company around me, so I thought, 'Right, you'd better look at me now because I've turned a different corner.' I made sure I did every interview and made sure I did every photo shoot, every cameraman got a picture of me. And I made sure I did every interview pissed as well."

As the festival wound down on the Sunday night, Rob hitched a lift back up north in the back of one of Oasis' Transit vans, in time for tour rehearsals with Take That on Monday. As Mark remembers, he was in no state to do anything the following day, and his condition only served to alienate other members of the group. "He was absolutely wasted – he'd obviously had a good time but he was knackered... it wound people up a little bit, y'know, 'Why do we have to stay around and work and he's off enjoying himself and he comes back like that?'" Howard was incensed by Rob's Glastonbury adventures:

"I thought it was tosserish... he was photographed, absolutely pissed, lying in a haystack and he just looked like a bag of shit, and everything like that reflected on us... he was a lazy bastard."

For the next three weeks, the other members of Take That did their best to ignore Rob's stories of new-found celebrity friends as they went on with rehearsals for the upcoming 20-date *Nobody Else* UK stadium tour. After his freestyle dancing for Oasis, Rob found the rigid choreography impossible to replicate – "They're your moves, not mine" – and his role within the band unacceptable. "I don't want to be one of Gary Barlow's backing dancers," he told Nigel during one of their confrontations. "I'll come to rehearsals, but I'll do it my own way." He began to talk openly within the camp about wanting to leave the band the following January, after the tour was finished and he'd banked £1 million for his efforts – Jan was already quietly sourcing a new manager for his solo exploits. To Rob's mind, the six months' notice he was offering should suffice, but Nigel's worries went far beyond the tour. Take That had just signed a £1 million deal with Arista in the US and Nigel foresaw the next two years as being dedicated to cracking the States. They couldn't make their initial in-roads as a five-piece only to return one member down in the New Year, just as they couldn't set out on tour with rumours of Robbie leaving the band rife or – worse still – have him leave midway through the dates. It became apparent that it was a 'now or never' situation, and it was Jason who acted as the catalyst.

Unlike Howard, who had sung lead on two songs and co-written others, Jason had always remained just a dancer within the band – Ian Levine even recalled being told not to waste time trying to get a vocal out of him in recording sessions. Yet as the second-oldest member of the band he had no time for Robbie's adolescent behaviour, not least if it was going to have a detrimental effect on everything he and the rest of Take That had worked so hard to achieve over the past five years.

The makeshift rehearsal rooms at the Territorial Army barracks in Stockport, Cheshire would be the last place the original Take That line-up were all together. On Thursday 13 July 1995, after a morning of more choreography followed by lunch – while the others ate from the healthy catering table Rob opted for a McDonalds meal – Jason made his feelings known. "If you're going, go now so we can get on with it." Rob took a piece of melon from the table, asked if he could take it with him, and made to leave. Standing in the doorway, he issued his own ultimatum. "Look, I'm going. No coming back. This is it." None of the rest of the band, his colleagues through all the back-breaking years of obscurity and success, said a word. Rob got into his car and was driven to his mum's new home. Once inside, he broke down and cried.

The following day, perhaps believing it to have been a bad row at worst, the band attempted to contact Rob and get him to rejoin rehearsals. He was already out enjoying his freedom in the South of France, celebrating George Michael's new multi-million-pound record deal with Paula Yates and Michael Hutchence in St Tropez. He asked George, himself a former boy band star with Wham!, whether he should leave for good; George agreed it was for the best. The decision made, Nigel acted fast – thousands of souvenir tour programs and posters were pulped, re-written and reprinted to excise all mention of Robbie, while the US edition of *Nobody Else* was redesigned to remove his face from the sleeve.

In the rehearsal space, someone found poetry Rob had written before he left. "The songs were about me and the other boys and how unhappy he was," admitted Nigel. "When I saw them, I was gob-smacked. They were clever lyrics."

The news of Rob's departure was broken in a statement released on 17 July that claimed he was "no longer able to give Take That the long-term commitment they needed." Gary was quoted as saying "The four of us are still 100 per cent committed to this band. We feel we owe it to the fans to carry on for as long as they want us here," and Mark refuted any thought of the group splitting with, "We love what we do so much and have so much to look forward to that we thought we couldn't possibly call it a day." Howard added "What's happened makes us more determined to put on a great show for the fans," while Jason's quote was pragmatic: "We'll all miss Rob, but we feel the only way to go now is forward." For now, even Rob was keeping to the script, telling the tabloids, "It was an incredibly hard decision to make and I hope the fans understand... I have decided to call it a day but I have only positive memories of Take That."

Back from France, Rob was believed to have stayed at the Camarthen Bay holiday camp in Wales (which was run by a friend of Pete's) for a week, before the tabloids tracked him down and he headed to London. The site manager told reporters, "He wanted to be left alone – he has been going through a tough time. But he was in good spirits and he wants to carry on singing and dancing as a solo star." The first of a slew of unsuitable offers came Rob's way: £130,000 to pose nude for the soft porn magazine *For Women*. He declined, but not without extracting some self-deprecating humour from the situation: "That's 65 grand an inch, or not..."

In August, as Take That achieved their first Number One as a quartet with the elegiac *Never Forget* and received good reviews on tour, the newly-solo Rob's "cheeky chappy" image took a battering. Small stories had cropped up over the past year hinting that partying was getting the better of his talent. In one instance, he'd tried to gatecrash a Radio One show; a BBC spokesperson said, "Robbie Williams didn't get into the studio – drunken members of Take That are very easy to spot." Just before the release of *Nobody Else*, it was reported that Robbie had been "banned from singing lead on the band's new album" because of mistakes made on their recent European "Pops" tour. "I gave Mark a couple of songs to go away and learn, and he came back and did them beautifully," Gary was quoted as saying. "I gave Robbie about 12 and, when he came back, he didn't even know half of any of them." Yet when a tabloid claimed Rob's fondness for cocaine and ecstasy had impaired his recent performances – "TAKE THAT SENSATION: WE HAD TO SACK DRUGS DAFT ROBBIE" – any pretence at shielding young fans from the awful truth was long gone. Rob's legal team immediately threatened to sue for defamation; Jan was door-stepped at home and declared herself "devastated" by the news.

Rob went into hiding at the Cheshire home of his new manager, recently appointed by Jan. Kevin Kinsella, another entrepreneur on the Manchester scene, planned to deflect the negative press and allow Rob time to rebuild his career out of the paparazzi's

A HUNDRED GRAND
UP FRONT:
ROBBIE AGREED TO
A WEEK'S WORK
PRESENTING ON
THE BIG BREAKFAST

view. On their first meeting, Rob burst into tears; "He was weeping for his career, for the life he had in that band," said Kevin. Rob spent weeks at the Kinsellas', lying around in his underwear and drinking as much as two bottles of vodka a day. (The bingeing was not a recent development – Rob was believed to have been downing a bottle daily before the final weeks of rehearsals with Take That.) Kevin's cure-all remedy for Rob's misery was work. He signed him up for a week's guest-presenting on Channel 4's suitably anarchic *The Big Breakfast* for £100,000 (paid up-front) and agreed a one-off deal for Rob to pose in underpants, high heels and a wig to promote 7-UP Light.

The day before the 7-UP stunt, Rob was brought face to face with the remaining members of Take That, when they separately handed out trophies at the National Television Awards. The two parties waved across the room at each other; Mark – who claimed to have cried when Rob left – said "It was obviously emotional, but we are getting on with our lives and he is getting on with his." Rob seemed to agree, if only with the first part of his comment; he was later found sobbing backstage.

In a cover feature for style magazine *The Face* Rob talked about his former existence positively – "Take That did a lot for me, moulded a huge part of my life and the whole base of where I'm going to go from here. Because school didn't – they did" – but had seemingly not begun to settle into his new life yet. "It's not been good, it's not good now. It's not bad, it has been bad... I don't feel great about myself right now." He added that he yearned for a girlfriend and domesticity; "I'm not going to find the real Robbie Williams jetting off to New York. I'm going to find him at home, where he hasn't been for six years." Rumours circulated that he would now make a move into musical theatre, taking the lead in either a West End revival of The Who's rock opera *Tommy* or Andrew Lloyd Webber's *Joseph and the Amazing Technicolour Dreamcoat*, a role played by Jason Donovan a few years earlier.

Still tagging along with Oasis when their schedule allowed, he accompanied them to the filming of *Top Of The Pops* at Elstree Studios in Hertfordshire one week, infiltrated the adjacent set of soap opera *EastEnders* and was later seen on screen, talking on the payphone in the Queen Vic. "It was spur of the moment... I was just hanging out and completely off my trolley. I just decided to take myself off for a walk and ended up on the *EastEnders* set where I said, 'Can I be an extra?'" Indeed, Rob's desperation to keep up with the Gallaghers saw him leading an increasingly unhealthy lifestyle down in the capital. Kevin received a call from record producer friend Nellee Hooper telling him to "Get Rob out of London or he'll be dead in three months." He was on a cycle of bingeing on food, drink and drugs, only stopping to dose himself up with sleeping pills to get some rest, then starting all over again. When Jan travelled down to London to see him, he'd pretend not to be home rather than face her in such a state: "I didn't want to see her. I was off my face."

Predictably, the ever-fickle teen readers of *Smash Hits*, who for years had laden Take That with as many gongs as they could carry – not least for "Best Haircut", singled out Rob as "Saddest Loser" at the 1995 Poll Winners Party while his old band won "Best Group in the world" for the fourth successive year.

Rob was becoming more than Kevin could handle, and they chose to dissolve their business arrangement, beginning a lengthy dispute over unpaid costs amounting to £400,000. Rob immediately rang his Glastonbury buddy Tim Abbott and engaged his management services with the words, "You got me in this mess, now get me out of it."

In an interview with Sunday broadsheet *The Observer* just before Christmas, the influence of the Gallaghers' working class rock'n'roll (not to mention predilection for illegal substances) was apparent in their wired protégé: "Britpop? It's great! ... I'm mad for any British youth movement. I mean, we invented Teddy Boys, Mods and Rockers, Punks and all that... I used to think indie music was a bunch of miserable people complaining, and because I was in Take That I thought that everybody had to be happy, and every message should be about love. But this year I've realised that the indie attitude's right... People are right to complain. And people should complain more and more." They were words at odds with those of the home-loving man interviewed by *The Face* some months earlier, but then Rob hadn't done well at achieving anything resembling domestic bliss quite yet. He did, however, experience a romantic reversal of fortunes late in the year when actress Patsy Kensit introduced him to her friend Jacqui Hamilton-Smith at a party thrown, paradoxically, by Nelle Hooper. (Rob would return the favour by hooking Patsy up with his friend Liam on a subsequent night out; they married a couple of years later and were divorced in 2000.) A make-up artist and the future Lady Colwyn, 28-year-old Jacqui was a society girl with her own connections to London's celebrity circles, and would become Rob's first proper girlfriend. Over the course of the next nine months they introduced each other to their families, holidayed in expensive, exotic resorts and set up home together in West London.

Tim recalls that Jacqui regularly cooked huge roast dinners which contributed to Rob's massive weight gain after leaving Nigel's regime (where non-diet fizzy drinks were a once-a-month treat). Having spent five years dancing for hours every day, "He could eat for England," said Tim. "He had no concept of diet... if there were a few spuds on the side of your plate, he'd be, 'Hey, have you finished with those?' We were amazed at what he could consume. And he'd always be looking at his watch, going, 'Oh, 11 o'clock – can we stop for coffee and cake?' He ran his day by food." Within months, Rob had added three stones to his frame, and childhood memories of being bullied over his size would increase his feelings of worthlessness and despair.

Adding to his troubles was his inability to start a solo career. Although Rob had tried to write and record new material throughout 1995 ("It was shit," claimed Kevin), the terms of his existing contract with RCA meant he would be unable to release anything unless it was on his old label, who he believed were currently more concerned with promoting Take That than developing his individual potential. He launched a legal bid in December to leave RCA's parent company BMG. Although a hearing date had been set for February the following year, the two parties eventually settled out of court and Rob withdrew his case – at a personal cost of £250,000 – with the prepared statement, "I now fully accept the validity and enforceability of my BMG recording contract. I remain a BMG artist."

He couldn't have foreseen it, but a momentous event on his 22nd birthday would put paid to any fresh hopes of becoming a priority artist for the label.

chapter 4

FREEDOM

THE INDUSTRY GOSSIP HIT THE TABLOIDS ON 12 FEBRUARY 1996: UNDER increased pressure since Robbie's departure, the remaining four members of Take That were preparing to split. A press conference was called for the following day and Gary Barlow broke the news:

"Unfortunately, the rumours are true. *How Deep Is Your Love?* is going to be our last single together, and the *Greatest Hits* is going to be our last album, and from today, there's no more..."

During the media Q&A session that followed, a journalist asked Gary, "Have you got a birthday message for Robbie? It's his birthday today." Gary's reply – "Is it? Oh..." – whether honest or not, signified the ongoing poor relations between the estranged parties.

Bookies rushed out their odds for the members' future successes. Gary was judged most likely to succeed, with odds of 6/4 from Ladbrokes on being the first to achieve a solo Number One. Robbie was next with 2/1 followed by Mark at 6/1, with Howard and Jason's chances pegged at only 50/1. William Hill were already offering 10/1 on Gary grabbing the 1996 Christmas Number One, while the inevitability of *How Deep Is Your Love?* hitting top spot was reflected in odds of only 1/10.

RCA announced that Gary and Mark would continue as solo artists on the label while Howard and Jason contemplated their futures, and that Robbie's solo material would only be released after singles from Gary and Mark.

Manager Tim Abbott was quick to articulate his client's dismay at yet another setback to his solo career – "Robbie's very upset. He feels patronised, not prioritized" – but was already in talks with a number of rival labels about buying Rob out of his RCA contract. Rob's sister Sally, who was suspended on full pay from her job with the Take That fanclub when her brother quit, was now made formally redundant too.

By summer, a £1.5million, four-album deal was on the table with EMI's Chrysalis label, brokered by EMI executive JF Cecillion (later the boss of Sega Europe), that agreed to compensate BMG several hundred thousand pounds for taking Rob off their books. Rob signed a confidentiality agreement that prevented him talking about his dealings with BMG and spent another £400,000 on legal fees for the handover.

His days as "a BMG artist" over, Rob relaunched himself with a press conference of his own held at the stroke of midnight on 27 June, the day his old contract was formally terminated. Noticeably overweight and clad in a long-sleeved red England T-shirt, he talked about "looking forward to being seen and heard as an artist", and his debut album, which he claimed would be entitled *The Show-Off Must Go On*, before unveiling his first single and the accompanying video.

The decision to cover George Michael's *Freedom*, originally a hit in December 1990, was not Rob's, and he was unhappy with the choice (as, apparently, was George).

"*Freedom* had been JF's idea," revealed Rob's new A&R man at Chrysalis, Chris Briggs.

"JF wanted something out as soon as possible because there had been such a long gap, any single would do... The sentiment of *Freedom* fitted Rob's situation. He kind of did it under sufferance, although I don't think it's anything like as awful as he thinks."

The lyrics of *Freedom* were drawn from George's experiences in Wham!, making them ideal to express Rob's feeling upon leaving Take That and going it alone:

"I was every little hungry schoolgirl's pride and joy/And I guess it was enough for me... But today the way I play the game has got to change... There's something deep inside of me/There's someone I forgot to be... "

In the video, a tanned if podgy Rob splashed around on a tropical beach and looked furious as he delivered the lyrics to camera (and indirectly to his enemies).

Rob bit his tongue on the subject of his former band-mates during the press conference, but later the same day excerpts from an interview with gay magazine *Attitude* were released to the press. In it, Rob referred to Gary, Howard and Jason as "selfish, arrogant and thick," adding, "I never fucking liked them." Within hours he issued an apology though: "I am disgusted with myself for saying what I said. I was feeling very bitter at the time about being frustrated by Gary's record company and I didn't mean what I said."

Rather than engineer another chart battle akin to Oasis's *Roll With It* versus Blur's *Country House* the previous August (which Blur won), RCA and Chrysalis staggered the first singles from Gary and Robbie; unconfirmed rumours were rife that Gary was allowed to go first as part of Rob's severance package.

Gary's *Forever Love* was an originally-written, mature piano ballad in the mould of *Back For Good* and, as the bookies' predicted, it went straight to Number One on Sunday 14 July. Gary's success was short-lived; he was dethroned after only a week by the heirs to Take That's pop crown, The Spice Girls. *Wannabe* stayed at Number One for eight weeks, scuppering Rob's chances of a debut solo Number One. *Freedom*, a polished pop track that emulated the sound of George Michael's original, entered the charts at Number Two on 28 July and sold over a quarter of a million copies.

As for Rob's other former bandmates, Mark Owen's ethereal debut single, *Child*, would peak at Number Three when released in November; Howard recorded solo material for BMG which was never released; and Jason failed to secure a deal.

Despite having proved to his critics and himself that he had an audience as a solo artist, Rob was still unhappy and drinking to excess. Like Kevin Kinsella before him, Tim Abbott felt himself unable to control Rob's alcoholic rages. At one hotel in Germany, Rob drank his minibar dry before wrecking his room (costs were estimated at £8,000), exposing himself to gathered guests and running naked around the hotel in search of a photographer. Tim even took to ringing Jan to complain, until she told him she'd had enough: "I don't want any more phone calls. I'm not his manager, I'm his mum."

Help was to arrive in an unlikely form. Elton John, himself a former drug addict and alcoholic, recognised Rob's behaviour as a cry for help (not least when the 22-year-old drank himself sick on champagne at one of his parties) and invited him to stay at his Windsor mansion to sort himself out.

"It took me 16 years to admit I needed help," Elton told the press. "Robbie went off the rails for about a year and a half. He's only very young with a lot of pressure on him. If I can put him on the right path, then I will do it because I think the world of him."

After a few weeks of round-the-clock care from Elton's staff, Rob began the first and most important part of the recovery process: admitting he had a problem. Jan was especially overjoyed; after closing down her florist shop, she had retrained as a drugs counsellor, but she knew that until Rob realised the extent of his addictions she would be unable to help him. "He admitted what the rest of us knew, and was able to get help."

Elton put Rob in touch with the therapist who had helped cure his addictions in the '80s, celebrity counsellor Beechy Colclough. His methods? "It's simple. I'll say to a patient, 'Keep doing what you're doing and you'll keep having what you've got...' Drinkers like drinking, but drinking doesn't like them, because it makes them behave abnormally... You've got to change the way the person feels."

Rob soon began to benefit from twice-weekly visits; "[He] was in great form when his treatment finished," noted Beechy.

Although Rob had left Take That with a personal fortune estimated at £1.5million, it was being drained away fast by legal fees and his expensive lifestyle; his credit cards were now permanently maxed-out. Creatively, he was struggling too. His first single had been a cover version, backed with remixes and an interview, and he was finding it difficult to write his own songs from scratch. "I'm learning from the very beginning and I haven't got any songs of any standard," he admitted. "I haven't got a statement song yet. I will have and it'll be blinding. The next [single] will be a song written by me."

JF Cecillion attempted to give him a helping hand though by teaming him up with a songwriter who could create hits to order. Desmond Child, the author of songs as varied as KISS's *I Was Made For Loving You*, Ricky Martin's *Livin' La Vida Loca* and The Baha Men's *Who Let The Dogs Out* was commissioned to write whole new tracks for Rob. Against his will, but under pressure from Tim, Rob was dispatched to Desmond's Miami home to record them. It was to be a short, unhappy marriage of their talents.

"Desmond does what Desmond does," said Rob. "They are guaranteed hits with Desmond... but I was raised in Stoke-on-Trent and I went in the pub and I have a different outlook on life from someone who's lived in Miami all his life, writing songs for Jon Bon Jovi... He does a job for certain people, but not for me."

Desmond presented Rob and Chris Briggs with three complete songs when they arrived in Florida; "Lyrically, the moment Desmond started talking... Rob's face, you should have seen it," recalled Chris. They worked on the tracks nonetheless, along with a song Rob had been tinkering with on the outward journey, but were unhappy with the demos they brought back to the UK. Only Rob's song, *Old Before I Die*, would survive.

Tim's support for the Miami experiment, added to the tabloids finding out about the supposedly secret meetings with Beechy, put more strain on their working relationship and Rob parted company with his third manager in 15 months.

"Tim's been a fantastic help to me over the past months [but] I want total artistic freedom in the creative direction of my album... We haven't fallen out and I know we'll continue to be friends," read his optimistic statement.

Abbott's company, Proper Management, issued a strong reply: "I would like to think

we could settle the problem of my claim without litigation but I am afraid that it seems inevitable that Rob's lawyers will shortly be hearing from mine."

Indeed they did. In addition to Kevin Kinsella's ongoing petition, Tim claimed over £1 million in unpaid commission. A few months earlier, Nigel Martin-Smith had lodged a sizeable writ at The High Court. He was suing for his cut of the royalties Rob earned after leaving Take That, a figure close to £80,000, plus 20 per cent of his "relevant" earnings until 2001 and 10 per cent thereafter until 2006. Rob was in dire need of new, sympathetic management and songwriting inspiration, if only to pay his court costs.

Jan would again guide her son's career, advising him to shop around for management this time rather than hooking up with someone who was simply "a top bloke and right on my level," as Rob had once described Tim. His accountant prepared a list and, after a series of meeting, with potential recruits, Rob realised he had immediately felt at ease in the company of management team David Enthoven and Tim Clark of IE Music. He was open about his addiction problems; they likened him to "a horse that's been abused and doesn't trust the people sent to look after him any more." David especially empathised with his situation. Both he and Tim had worked in the music industry for over 30 years, managing and promoting bands including T.Rex and Roxy Music, but massive success had led David down a similar path to Rob. He became a cocaine and heroin addict in the late '70s and was broke and reduced to living with his mother before he managed to enter rehab and successfully restart his career in the early '90s.

After their first meeting, they watched Rob successfully host the 1996 MTV Europe Music Awards at Alexandra Palace in north London (thus making amends for his after-show overkill two years earlier) and decided to take him onto their roster. They then met again at Rob's London flat ("I was just this coke and beer monster... unwashed with a beard coming through and big hair," recalled Rob later) where he played them demos of songs he'd been working on. David's assessment was kinder that Kevin's – "It was all very average... there was probably one song in there that was reasonably interesting" – but not much more hopeful. Eager to please, Rob suggested something else: "D'you want to hear some of my poetry?" It was to be the turning point for Rob's songwriting career.

"Tim and I looked at each other and knew instantly that it could work," said David. "From that moment on I thought, 'Well, that's easy. All we've got to do now is find him somebody to mill that into music."

While Rob's ideas for collaborators were a little too aspirational – he told Chris he wanted to work with his idol, Frank Sinatra – Tim and David were a little more realistic. They put out the word that they were looking for a musician, and began "wading through endless shit", before two tapes by someone called Guy Chambers were sent to them from two different contacts. A pianist since the age of five, Guy had since learnt an array of instruments and joined a number of bands. He was signed to Virgin for a time with little-known synth-rockers Hambi and the Dance before touring on keyboards for The Teardrop Explodes, The Waterboys and World Party. He then fronted a band of his own, indie types The Lemon Trees, who released the album *Open Book* on MCA in 1993, before splitting. "I wasn't a good enough singer... I wasn't Mr Charisma on stage," said Guy. "I needed to find a partner who could be the pop star I couldn't be."

After Rob's previous, unsuccessful attempts to co-write, with Oasis' producer Owen Morris (which only produced b-side *Cheap Love Song*) and Elastica's dancer/keyboardist Anthony Genn (who was credited as a co-writer of album track *Clean*), David and Tim were cautious that nothing should jeopardise the potential arrangement with Guy. Ahead of their first meeting, on 8 January 1997, Guy was advised not to refer to Rob as "Robbie" and not to try and be his friend. But their working relationship was to be easier than anyone could have expected. "I knew immediately [when] Rob walked into the studio and opened his mouth that he was really great," said Guy. "He had all these great lyrical ideas... the combination of us was very powerful."

On the first day alone they wrote four songs, future single *South Of The Border*, album tracks *Killing Me* and *Life Thru A Lens* and b-side *Teenage Millionaire*. The next day they reworked an old Lemon Trees song into single *Lazy Days* with the aid of new lyrics, and took just 20 minutes to create *Angels*. Immediately afterwards, Guy developed a severe headache. "I think he made himself ill with excitement," said Rob. "He knew how good it was... but didn't quite dare believe it." When they aired the new tracks for Tim and David, the managers were ecstatic. "It just worked instantly," said David. "All this repressed energy... We thought it was pop heaven."

Angels had actually begun life a few weeks earlier, in a Dublin pub. Rob was on a short pre-Christmas break when he met songwriter Ray Heffernan in The Globe. They carried on drinking back at Ray's home where he played Rob a song he'd been working on called *Angels Instead*. They recorded the song, first on a Dictaphone, then in a studio, arranged by Westlife's manager Louis Walsh, with a dance backing track. Delighted with their demo, Rob insisted that Ray should join his band. Ray duly followed him to London a few days later (Rob was away) then to Jan's home (where his presence freaked Rob out). After he left, he was contacted by IE Music and offered a one-off payment of £10,000 to renounce any future claims for royalties on the track, which had already been selected for Rob's album. Despite claiming that "the verse and the verse melody was mine," Ray accepted, and the song was credited to 'R Williams and G Chambers'.

The songs still had to be demoed and recorded. The first test of the new material would come in the form of a taxi driver who recognised Rob as he drove him to the studio.

"[He] asked what I was up to these days, so I said I was just going to try something out with somebody new." A few hours later Rob took a cab home again and by chance got the same driver. "I gave him the tape of *Angels* and said, 'Play that.' He did, and said 'That's Number One, that is'."

Having enjoyed working with Steve Power on The Lemon Trees' album, Guy asked him to co-produce Rob's record. Between them they built a band around him and began to demo and record the material for release later in the year.

Finally, Rob's career had received the boost he'd been waiting for, yet by now the persuasive power of Beechy's counselling had waned and Rob's relationship with Jacqui had ended. No matter that he had written *Angels*, the "statement song" he'd been longing for, Rob's fondness for alcohol had returned with a vengeance and he spent much of the recording process lying drunk beneath the mixing desk. By his own admission, he "didn't know how to stop drinking".

NOT EVEN RECORDING ANGELS, THE "STATEMENT SONG" HE'D YEARNED FOR COULD TEMPER ROB'S DRINKING

chapter 5

LOVING ANGELS

'**O**LD BEFORE I DIE*, THE ONLY FINISHED TRACK FROM ROB'S POST-*FREEDOM* solo sessions, was slated for release as Rob's second single in March 1997. JF Cecillion had spent a considerable amount on securing Desmond Child's cooperation and wanted to see a return on his investment, but Rob, his management and the band weren't so sure. Secretly, Guy and Steve re-recorded the "cheesy" original during the album sessions until everyone was satisfied that this version was in keeping with Rob's new material, at which point they played it to JF. He was impressed enough to allow that to be the version released, and the date was moved back to April.

Now drenched with scuzzy, "indie"-sounding guitars, the bluesy and Oasis-indebted *Old Before I Die* mirrored the success of *Freedom* and peaked at Number Two, behind R Kelly's sentimental *Space Jam* anthem *I Believe I Can Fly*. With a decidedly un-rock'n'roll sentiment, the lyrics of *Old Before I Die* took stock of Rob's current problems ("Tonight I'm gonna live for today/So come along for the ride") and held out hope for a sober future ("I hope I live to relive the days gone by"), but a throwaway line at the end of the second chorus would return to haunt him: "Am I straight or gay?"

Within weeks, Gary Barlow scored his second solo Number One with *Love Won't Wait*, an up-tempo version of a track Madonna wrote and only demoed for her 1994 album *Bedtime Stories*. Gary's first album, *Open Road*, was released the following month and went straight to the top of the charts, selling 350,000 copies within weeks.

By now, Rob's renewed taste for partying – as opposed to his new music – was the talk of the tabloids, as was his new romance with ex-soap opera starlet Anna Friel. Seen staggering from nightclubs in cahoots with Simply Red singer Mick Hucknall one week and smooching Anna on the balcony of a Rome hotel room the next, Rob was back on the path to self-destruction. The extent of his ill-health became evident when he turned up to play at the all-star Soccer Six charity tournament in west London on 18 May. After visiting Anna on location in Ireland filming the BBC TV movie *All For Love*, he had gone on a three-day bender around London. Despite scoring two goals alongside Mark Owen in a team captained by the Lightning Seeds' Ian Broudie, one onlooker described him as "bleary eyed and vomiting", noting that "his eyes were bloodshot and he seemed to be talking gibberish... The most energetic thing he did was bare his bum at the crowd."

Chrysalis were quick to deflect attention from any addictive behaviour, a spokesman claiming: "Robbie was sick the whole night before – we all think he was a bit of a hero". But pop columnist Matthew Wright of *The Mirror* was unconvinced and called Tim Clark. What Tim told him was intended to be in confidence, but Wright ran the story as an exclusive headlined, "BOOZED UP ROB OUT OF CONTROL". Tim revealed that the decision had already been made for Rob to go into a residential rehab centre, saying his long battle with drugs and drink had left him on the brink of suicide: "We knew Rob had an addiction problem when we took him on... But you cannot make someone sort

themselves out. He is absolutely determined to go in to treatment and sort himself out."

Jan travelled down to London to help take care of her son, telling reporters, "Robert is poorly. He has a drink problem... The whole situation from Take That to the present day has been the major contribution to his problems."

Days later, a Sunday tabloid ran an interview with Rob in which he said, "I think I'm going to die before I'm 30. I don't know why I've just got this feeling that it will turn out like that... That's why I try to live each day as fully as I possibly can."

Tim and Dave chose Clouds House in Wiltshire for Rob's rehab. The treatment centre supports 38 live-in patients with a maximum stay of 42 continuous days. The regime is simple: patients share rooms, do their own washing-up and are treated as equals, regardless of celebrity or wealth, while undertaking a 12-step program to beat their addictions. The 12 steps involve admitting to an addiction, admitting to needing help in beating it, asking for that help from a higher power and apologising to the people who your addiction has affected. A lapsed Catholic, Rob didn't choose God as his higher power, but Elvis Presley. He now precedes live performances with Alcoholics Anonymous' adopted 'Serenity Prayer', but instead of addressing it to God, he directs it to the King of Rock'n'Roll (who died prematurely because of his own battles with drink and drugs): "Elvis grant me the serenity to accept the things I cannot change, the courage to change things I can and the wisdom to know the difference."

Except for a short break to film a video for his third single, *Lazy Days*, Rob stayed for the full six weeks, emerging in mid-July. He was effusive in his praise for Clouds. "It's the sort of place that when I have kids I'd send them there for finishing school," he told homeless charity magazine *The Big Issue*. "In the past two months I haven't had a drink. Tomorrow I might have a drink. But today I haven't had a drink and tomorrow I probably won't." He also revealed he had begun to pray for his four former bandmates, even though he still didn't like Gary. "I don't know why I dislike Gary. Well, I do, but I don't know why I can't get over it."

With Rob unavailable for the usual press duties, the '60s-influenced, almost psychedelic *Lazy Days* ("The world can change in a second so/I find the sunshine beckons me/To open up the gate and dream") reached only Number Eight days after his release. But Rob had bigger problems. Less than a week after leaving Clouds he returned to The High Court to defend himself against Nigel Martin-Smith's claim for non-payment of commission.

Nigel's lawyer described Take That as: "A boys' band, marketed at young girls. They were designed to please rather than shock. They were the sort of boys that girls could take home to their mums for tea." He outlined Nigel's "unwritten code" of behaviour: to not go out without a chaperone present, to maintain a presentable image at all times, to be committed to the band and to appear approachable yet unattached. He added that by 1994 Rob "began to behave in a manner out of step, out of synchronisation with the rest of Take That ... He began to develop a taste for glamorous and flamboyant parties, alcohol and narcotics. Williams was turning up at rehearsals hungover and unprepared to rehearse." He also revealed that the other members held crisis meetings to discuss how they could "sort Robbie Williams out". Outside the court,

LEGAL ACTIONS
AND COURT CASES
WERE TO DOG ROB
FOR YEARS

Rob – looking slender in an Alexander McQueen suit – refused to allow the situation to affect his post-Clouds glow: "I feel fantastic. I'm in great shape. I feel good."

When Nigel took the stand later in the trial, he told the court that Rob's behaviour had caused "a terrible atmosphere" within the band which left Mark "close to collapse". "Jason wanted Robbie to go and Gary was not keen on him staying. They were the band leaders and weren't prepared to go on with him." Nigel also claimed he told them Rob couldn't be sacked, but he could be "encouraged to leave". Rob's reaction was to tell reporters outside the court, "After this I'm off to become a member of the clergy".

Judgement was reserved until October allowing Rob back on the promotional trail, but his fourth single, *South Of The Border*, fared poorly, peaking at Number 14. With a swaggering rhythm reminiscent of The Steve Miller Band classic *The Joker* and lyrics explicitly about his Class-A addictions ("I know a freaky little lady name of Cocaine Katie/She makes my temperature freeze... She'll bring you to your knees") it was an unconvincing attempt to sound like his new best friends Liam and Noel Gallagher and didn't bode well for the album.

Having opted not to include *Freedom* – Rob told interviewers he'd made George Michael quite enough money already – the album, now entitled *Life Thru A Lens*, was finally released on 29 September with three singles of diminishing success to its credit. Despite attempts by his PRs to get journalists to start referring to him as Rob, the name "Robbie Williams" was too deeply etched into the nation's psyche for a more mature rebrand. Without ever intending to, Rob had acquired a stage name just like his Dad.

Opening with *Lazy Days*, *Life Thru A Lens*' title track came next. A bitter, if witty, sketch of the It girls and celebrity socialites Rob had found himself among over the past two years ("Fashion tardis down at *Quo Vadis*... I'm talking football, she's talking *Ab Fab*"), it was Britpop-by-numbers. The third track was *Ego A Go Go*: "Ego a go go/Now you've gone solo... Do you still hate me/Could you offer an apology?" he snarled over an Acid Jazz-y backing. "I can't lie – it's about one of the boys," Rob admitted.

Angels was next, offering an odd change of pace midway through the record with its *Imagine*-style piano and serious tone. "I believe you have guardian angels and Auntie Jo and my Grandad are looking after me," explained Rob; Rob Heffernan claimed it was originally about a baby his former girlfriend miscarried.

South Of The Border and *Old Before I Die* ("The first and last song I will ever write with Desmond Child") followed, then came "a tribute to the most important person in my life – my mum." The folky, almost acoustic *One Of God's Better People* was in the same heartfelt vein as *Angels*, if less bombastic ("It must hurt to see your favourite man/Lose himself again and again... I know that you're my only friend').

Adding to the schizophrenia of the album, the rabble-rousing statement of intent *Let Me Entertain You* followed ("You gotta get high before you taste the lows"). While memories of the video will forever link it to KISS, ironically it had far more in common with Bon Jovi's Desmond Child-penned *Living On A Prayer* period.

Then came *Killing Me*, an oddly unbalanced track with moments of swooning Beatles-y strings and more contemplation of addiction ("The joke's on me/And I don't wanna laugh"). The jaunty, Britpoppy *Clean* served as an antidote, extolling the virtues of sobriety – "There was a time/When crazy days would start with wine... But I'm clean... Don't have to wean myself off of nothing". Ironically, Rob admits he was, "completely out of it when I wrote this".

Baby Girl Window completed the triptych of ballads and appeared to end the album. Rob wrote it "for my friend Sam[antha] Beckinsale about her dad, Richard, who died when she was 12". Richard Beckinsale – also the father of Hollywood actress Kate – who can still be seen on TV in repeats of the classic sitcoms *Porridge* and *Rising Damp*, died from a heart attack in March 1979 at the age of 31. As well as acting he wrote poetry, and an anthology his wife Judy Loe published posthumously, *With Love*, contains the phrases "Baby girl widow", "With my rainbow in the shadow/Cast your sunbeams down on me" and "fingermarks around my soul" alluded to in the *Baby Girl Window* lyrics.

Almost 10 minutes after the end of the song, hidden track *Hello Sir* begins, the poem about Rob's unhappy schooldays. It's possibly the only moment on this or any album when the "Robbie" persona takes a back seat to the real Rob; he sounds close to tears as he recites the words over a sparse piano melody that recalls *Fitter, Happier* from Radiohead's album *OK Computer*, released a few months earlier.

It's a record which has aged well, sounding better now than it did upon release at the height of Britpop when it seemed contrived and derivative in context, and the sharpness and honesty of the lyrics have since become more apparent. (The thank-yous on the sleeve encompassed Nigel and Take That, the Kinsellas and the Gallaghers, and had a Cloudsian sense of goodwill about them.) Reviews at the time were mixed, however, and sales were slow. *Life Thru A Lens* debuted on the album chart at Number 11, behind new releases from old-timers Bob Dylan, The Rolling Stones, Elton John and Chris De Burgh, and slipped down to 29 the following week. EMI remained confident of future success, saying that although it wasn't "flying out [of the shops] at the moment... it's a massive release waiting to happen."

Rob set out on tour in support of the album, playing over-18s student union venues far smaller than he'd been used to in the latter days of Take That. The same fans turned out (albeit less of them), waving decidedly post-pubescent banners reading "SHOW US YOUR KNOB, ROB" and "ROBBIE, SHAG ME!" The short sets were culled from *Life Thru A Lens* plus covers: an irreverent punky version of *Back For Good* and a faithful rendition of David Bowie's *Kooks* (about his then-wife Angie and their son Zowie, now better known as Duncan). Where album reviews had been tepid, live reviews were full of praise: "His music and his performance mark him as a showman in the tradition of David Bowie, Alice Cooper and Meat Loaf," wrote a reviewer from *The Times*.

Whatever sensitivity his solo lyrics may have revealed, Rob was back playing at being Robbie, the boorish bad boy of pop, delivering encores naked but for a guitar and dropping barbs about his former bandmates between songs.

By 20 November the scales of justice had tipped against his favour yet again. Rob was ordered to pay Nigel £90,000 at The High Court, plus damages for breach of contract and commission on other sums earned since he left Take That, under the terms of his old management agreement. It was estimated that the eventual figure could

reach £1 million. With Rob away on tour in Europe, Chrysalis announced their intention to appeal against the costs.

Ecstatic live reviews still weren't selling the long-player, and industry insiders were quick to predict that Rob's four-album deal was in trouble. By current standards, a flop record and under-performing singles would indeed be the death knell for a newly-launched act, irrespective of their heritage. Chrysalis were keen to advertise the album on TV to increase sales but Rob's management team, mindful of the effect this would have on his credibility, persuaded them to bide their time. Tim and David were placing their faith in the song chosen as Rob's Christmas single, believing it would give the album the push it needed to make good on JF Cecillion's expensive investment.

Angels was released on 1 December, with an evocative black and white video that stripped away the showmanship to reveal Rob as a singer, pure and simple. The taxi driver who'd predicted a Number One was wrong – in a competitive festive market it entered the charts at only Number Seven. By the following week, bolstered by 1,800 airings a week on radio stations across the country, it rose two places and would hang around long enough to become the most-played song of 1998 (not to mention a karaoke classic and popular choice at funeral services). Most importantly of all, it meant that the album started to fulfil its potential.

Nominated for two Brit Awards – for Best British Male Artist and Best British Single for *Old Before I Die* – Rob attended the 1998 ceremony to duet with his "hero" Tom Jones. He was modest about comparisons ("I wasn't going to be able to out-sing Tom... my voice sounds like a girl's compared to his") and even though Finley Quaye beat him to the Best Male trophy and All Saints' *Never Ever* took Best Single, Rob stole the show. The duet was a medley of songs from the enormously successful British film *The Full Monty*, about unemployed Sheffield steel workers stripping to make money. While not adverse to public nudity, Rob kept his clothes on – a fitted leather suit that was supposed to pay homage to a younger Tom but was more evocative of Elvis Presley's *'68 Comeback Special* outfit. They sang excerpts from Steve Harley and Cockney Rebel's *Make Me Smile (Come Up And See Me)*, Tom's own *You Can Leave Your Hat On* and Wilson Pickett's *Land Of 1000 Dances*. Like Take That's Beatles medley three years earlier, it was all anyone could talk about afterwards. The live track was hastily added as a B-side to the single version of *Let Me Entertain You* which, aided by its pyrotechnical KISS tribute video, reached Number Three in March – Rob's highest chart placing in almost a year.

Work soon began on a second album. Rob and Guy were on holiday in Jamaica to write new material when they were called with the news that the first album had now sold 300,000 copies in the UK and achieved platinum status. Despite months of hard work on his sobriety – before the Brits, he told reporters he was going to resist the free alcohol at the ceremony and would instead "drink tea and eat cucumber sandwiches with my mother" – Rob couldn't help but celebrate with champagne. It wasn't until they received another call to tell them it was fast approaching double-platinum that he stopped, realising what he could be about to throw away, because on 12 April 1998, over six months after it was first released, *Life Thru A Lens* finally made it to Number One.

ROB'S DUET WITH
TOM JONES STOLE
THE SHOW AT THE
1998 BRIT AWARDS.

chapter 6

SHE'S THE
ONE

BEFORE GLASTONBURY 1995, EVEN BEFORE MOONING ON MTV EUROPE, Rob had publicly defied his manager's rules. At a party to celebrate the end of Take That's European "Pops" tour in spring 1995, he arrived arm-in-arm with TV actress Samantha Beckinsale in a deliberate attempt to flaunt Nigel Martin-Smith's strict "No Girlfriends" decree. Both were tight-lipped on the nature of their relationship, Samantha only admitting "I love him to bits", but they would remain on good terms long enough for him to include *Baby Girl Window* on *Life Thru A Lens* more than two years later. The art of staying friends with exes would not come easily to Rob thereafter.

Rob's relationship with Jacqui Hamilton-Smith first came to light when he accompanied her to Cheltenham for her grandmother's funeral in late January 1996. "I've only known Robbie for three weeks but I adore him," she declared, oddly using his stage name. "He's brilliant and we have a great time. We see each other as often as we can. Robbie is a very talented boy. The reason he left Take That was that he's different from the others and he wanted to do his own thing."

Their meeting couldn't have come at a better time. Increasingly estranged from his mother ("You go into therapy and they tell you it's all your parents' fault"), fighting RCA for his artistic freedom and finding himself a figure of fun in the tabloids, Rob needed the emotional support that he wasn't getting from manager Tim Abbott; 28-year-old Jacqui happily supplied it. She had already passed the most important test: tea with Nan.

Always happy to talk to the papers about her beloved grandson, Betty revealed "Robbie and Jacqui came round to tea. I had no idea who she was. I just said straight out to her, 'What's your name, duck?' She was so pretty and so polite. But I had no idea she was aristocracy. They just sat in my living room, drinking Coke. It wasn't until I read it in the papers that I realised she was a Lady. I nearly had a fit. I felt so embarrassed that I had called her duck. Any girl who gets Robbie is very lucky. He is the light of my life."

A couple of weeks after Take That had announced their split, Rob flew by Concorde to Barbados to join Jacqui at her father's villa. They were reunited at the airport, where they were seen "French-kissing, necking and almost undressing each other" in Arrivals before "frolicking on the beach and romping in the waves". Pursued down the sands by reporters, Rob sounded optimistic about his new romance: "Jacqui is tops. We're very much in love... I wouldn't want anyone to spoil this. It's perfect." Jacqui was a little more realistic – "Who knows how long it will last?" – but jokingly proposed to him on 29 February. Rob declined the offer, worried that she might be serious.

Jacqui swiftly revamped Rob's laddish wardrobe, replacing the Oasis-esque T-shirts and fishing hats with the suits and upmarket labels he still favours today, and introduced him to west London living. Rob bought a £200,000 flat in Maida Vale near her house, and Jacqui soon moved in with him. Most importantly of all, she appeared to love him unconditionally, allowing or perhaps in therapy speak "enabling" him to gain weight and

CHAPTER OPENER:
ROB AND ALL SAINT'
NICOLE APPLETON
HAD A TRAUMATIC
RELATIONSHIP.

RIGHT: ANNA FRIEL
– ANOTHER FUN
BUT SHORT-LIVED
ROMANCE FOR ROB

flattered by the gesture. Nicole asked her manager to get his number but she didn't dare to call until, a few days later, the story about Rob dating Denise reached the papers. As a kind of revenge, Nicole went out and got drunk, and then decided to call him. After a false start, when Charlie screened the call and told her Rob was out, he called back and invited her to the studio where he was recording new material. She arrived late, but Rob had saved them both a roast dinner and they ate together before he returned to the studio to record some vocals. Afterwards, they went to the local pub and got drunk, shared their first kiss in the snow outside, then returned to the farmhouse/studio to crash out – Nicole slept in her knickers and T-shirt. Early the next morning she left to film a video and that afternoon Rob called to say, "I had a really good time last night."

She didn't hear from him again for a week, when he rang to ask her to take him home from a party in North London. When Nicole arrived, he was "lying on the couch... [looking] as if he had been to hell and back". She took him back to his flat, and stayed with him for the next few days. They spent New Year's Eve apart, but by 2 January she had been snapped leaving his home and the secret was out. (When the Brit nominations were announced little over a week later, a profile of All Saints revealed that Nicole's ideal man was actually Liam Gallagher.)

With both Rob and Nicole on relentless promotional schedules it was always difficult for them to see each other, although they could sometimes meet in hotels when their paths crossed. At the end of March, having been seeing Rob for only three months, Nicole suspected she might be pregnant when on a trip to Vancouver, Canada. Melanie had also missed a period so the friends took pregnancy tests together – both were positive. Nicole rang Rob immediately to tell him. "I'm really happy about it," he told her. "It's what I want." She and Mel still had to break the news to their manager – Mel volunteered to go first, as they stopped over in Los Angeles en route to Australia. He went ballistic, and called a crisis meeting when they arrived in Australia, telling the girls that "the band is in danger of collapsing". As band leader Shaznay Lewis ranted at Mel, Nicole revealed that she was pregnant too. "I would have expected this of Nicole," said Shaznay, "but not of... Melanie".

Rob remained supportive, and after the promotion was done and Nicole was back in the UK he took her to meet Nan. He put his hands on Nicole's stomach and told Betty, "This baby is going to save my life." If their child was a girl he wanted to call it Grace, and he wrote an eponymous song about her for his new album – "Grace/I'm not yet born/Come embrace/A soul that's torn".

Pressure from her record label began to wear down Nicole's decision to carry the baby; they rang her mother and told her Rob was "bad news". Their manager convinced her sister Natalie – herself a single mother – that the baby would mean the end of the band, and it became plain that Nicole was being asked to chose between being a mother and being in All Saints. Exhausted by another promotional trip, this time to New York, she was taken into a meeting with the label and told an abortion could be arranged for the very next day. Feeling like she had no option, she unhappily agreed to go.

When she told Rob, he flew out immediately on Concorde to be by her side, asking only "Are you sure that's what you want?" The doctor was unsympathetic and the

After his affair with Nicole Appleton, Rob was linked with sometime TV presenter Tanya Strecker, but he says they were just "friends".

procedure excruciating; Nicole was in agony for weeks afterwards and lost an alarming amount of weight. Another doctor told her the operation had been inappropriate for a four-month-old foetus, and that tissue had been left behind that her body was trying to expel. Worse still, it might have left her unable to conceive again in future.

They never discussed the operation, and within weeks Rob proposed to Nicole as she returned to the UK from Japan, crying when she accepted and giving her an emerald-cut diamond ring. Jan gave her approval: "He's always looked forward to having a wife and family. I don't think he could have made a better choice."

But when Nicole was away in Brazil mere weeks later, Rob rang her to end the relationship. Broken-hearted, Nicole contemplated suicide by walking into the sea to drown herself but when she returned to the UK Charlie called to reassure her that Rob was still in love with her. The couple met again in London and were soon reunited and re-engaged only to split again on Christmas Day, after Rob's drinking returned to pre-Clouds House levels.

Rob attempted reconciliation via the media, telling the audience at a Newcastle Arena show, "I want to talk about Nicki," and replying to their supportive boos with "No, no, I need love too..." Nicole had attended the 1999 Brit Awards with Fun Lovin' Criminals' frontman Huey Morgan a few days earlier, and Rob had drowned his sorrows in vodka before leaving early. His ploy worked, and they were seen together again in March, when he entertained Nicole by dropping a paparazzo's car keys down a drain. She said "I love Rob and always will. What we had was a lot more special than anybody else I know."

Yet less than six weeks later Nicole's tone had turned decidedly bitter, and her carefully-chosen words ensured another reconciliation would never happen. "It's over," she told the tabloids. "Robbie's life isn't real. He actually leads a pathetic life. Robbie was too unstable for me and I hope he reads that. The constant rowing and his lifestyle drove us apart. I would never have children with him. He is too crazy. The father of my children would have to lead a normal life."

After his traumatic affair with Nicole, by his own admission Rob didn't have "a relationship with anybody as boyfriend and girlfriend for over two years." He met leggy, sometime TV presenter Tanya Strecker through her stepfather, his manager David, but claimed "we weren't going out with each other, we were friends. We never committed to a relationship." He attempted to woo Irish singer Andrea Corr after meeting her at the 1999 Brit Awards, with a bouquet of roses and a note attached quoting a Corrs' lyric: "What can I do to make you love me?" She reportedly failed to respond and soon received a cactus in place of the bouquet. He was linked to the most successful female stars of the moment – teen pop sensation Billie and Australian soap stars-turned-singers Natalie Imbruglia and Kylie Minogue – but love would elude Rob again and again.

"I loved Rob but our relationship was always on the verge of ending," said Nicole. It would later emerge that they had already split up once before she knew she was pregnant. "To this day I still don't know... the real reason why our relationship ended." She would be hurt again years later when, having given birth to her son Gene by new boyfriend Liam Gallagher, Rob didn't contact her to offer his congratulations.

"JUMP ON BOARD, FEEL THE HIGH..." ROB AND KYLIE RECORDING AND PERFORMING TOGETHER PREDICTABLY TRIGGERED RUMOURS OF ROMANCE.

chapter 7

COME
UNDONE

WHILE HIS LOVELIFE IMPLODED ROB'S CAREER WAS EXCEEDING expectations, and even offering him the chance to atone for earlier indiscretions. There was no Glastonbury Festival in 1996 and Rob was in Clouds House throughout the 1997 event. When the time came for organiser Michael Eavis to book the acts for the 1998 festival, he invited Rob to attend again and perform alongside Bob Dylan, Tony Bennett, Foo Fighters, Blur, Pulp and Primal Scream. The prospect terrified him, he told journalists beforehand. This would be his biggest show to date – bigger even than any Take That concert – with Glastonbury attracting over 100,000 people annually. It would also be an opportunity to lay to rest the image of his shambolic dancing jester on stage with Oasis three years earlier. He confirmed his appearance and, accompanied by Jan and Nicole (Glastonbury was post-engagement and pre-Brazil), arrived on site on Saturday 27 June, sober, in a Range Rover with blacked-out windows. Unlike in previous years he kept to himself backstage, only offering audiences to pre-booked members of the press. When the time came for him to perform, in a late afternoon slot, he was driven the 100 yards to the production area (1998 was the second rained-out Glastonbury in a row).

As per his recent shows the intro music was John Williams' *Star Wars* theme, swiftly followed by the brazen opening chords of *Let Me Entertain You*. And then the words he'd been bandying around in pre-festival interviews: "My name is Robbie Williams, and I am shitting myself!"

Whatever nerves Rob may have felt beforehand, Robbie displayed none of them, running through his tried-and-tested live set like a man on a mission to reclaim his credibility from Glastonbury's uneasy-to-impress punters. (Keanu Reeves' dreadful hobby-band Dogstar played one year, in a similar time slot, and were soon showered with bottles from the cynical masses who had arrived out of curiosity.) It was a triumph, from the thrashy *Back For Good* to the finale of *Angels* which everyone present sang along with, hardened crusties and sceptical scenesters alike.

Afterwards, he sat exhausted on his tourbus with Jan and Nicole, appearing to be in a state of shock. He didn't toast his success, he simply took it in – slowly. On Monday, *The Guardian* declared that he had been "the biggest draw of the afternoon... somewhat surprisingly" and noted that "nearly all [the crowd] were converted by the end. Williams' self-deprecating wit... and his party-piece punk version of Take That's *Back For Good* made an hour zip by." Rob was reborn, and Robbie had won a whole new audience.

The next test of his popularity would be the first single from the second album. Could his luck last? Was the Williams-Chambers partnership a fixture or a fluke? *Millennium* denied the latter and provided Rob's first solo Number One in September. Using a hypnotic strings sample from John Barry's *You Only Live Twice* Bond theme, it was the first of his songs to allude to romantic relationships rather than addiction, friends and family.

"Round and round in circles/Live a life of solitude/'Til we find ourselves a partner/Someone to relate to/Then we slow down/Before we fall down."

It was apparent that, problems apart, his time with Nicole was offering him the salvation he had craved in *Angels* – when he originally wrote the song, at least. *Millennium* ousted All Saints' *Bootie Call* from the top spot on 13 September and stayed for a week before Mel B from the Spice Girls' collaboration with Missy Elliott, *I Want You Back*, took over.

It had taken Rob two years longer than Gary Barlow to get his first Number One but Gary's solo career was already stuttering. The singles from his second album, *Stronger* and *For All That You Want*, charted at Number 16 and Number 24 before disappearing; the album itself, *Twelve Months, Eleven Days,* would peak at Number 35 in October. By marked contrast, Rob's *I've Been Expecting You* entered at Number One on 1 November, and would return to the top twice more over the coming months.

Continuing the Bond motif of *Millennium* in the cover image and title was perhaps a deliberate distraction from the real meaning of the record; had Nicole given birth to their baby, it would have been born around the release date. It's also an album recorded, if not written, with stadium-sized crowds in mind – it sounds huge, more ambitious and lyrically ambiguous than its predecessor, without much doubt as to its future success.

Anthemic opener *Strong* was another confessional in the mould of *Life Thru A Lens* – "Life's too short to be afraid/So take a pill to numb the pain/You don't have to take the blame" – with undertones of Oasis' *Don't Look Back In Anger*. The epic, electronic *No Regrets*, comprising Rob's feelings towards his old bandmates ("I felt so vacant/You treat me like a child"), followed, with backing vocals from new friends Neil Tennant of the Pet Shop Boys and The Divine Comedy's Neil Hannon.

After *Millennium* came *Phoenix From The Flames*, the album's first ballad. With a piano melody, deliberately or not it recalled *A Million Love Songs* before going honky-tonk in the middle. Like *Angels,* it was about redemption: "Silence shields the pain so you say nothing... Shelter me from pain/I always wanna feel this way."

The rocky *Win Some, Lose Some* opened with Nicole's off-key voice as recorded onto a novelty keyring for Rob ("I love you, ba-by...") and offered a requiem for a relationship that wasn't even over yet: "She touched my face and called me her lover/I never thought that I'd need another... You win some, you lose some/Now it's gone."

Grace followed, an easy listening track with a French feel that's a diversion from the lyrics about the unborn baby: "My heart is starved of love... I know I've sold my soul/I'm going to earn it back now... I have got so much to give you."

Jesus In A Camper Van harked back to *Lazy Days* territory, both musically and lyrically ("And now it's four in the mornin'... No one can shoot but everybody's scoring"), while the lovely *Heaven From Here* offered up the second straight ballad ("We are love and I just wanna hold you near/Know no fear/We will see heaven from here") with a vocal melody reminiscent of Sam Brown's massive 1988 hit *Stop*.

The spiky *Karma Killer* could almost have been an outtake from Pulp's *Different Class* with its sweeping strings and Jarvis Cocker inflections, while the lyrics were another dig at the litigious Nigel Martin-Smith: "You could prop up the bar in hell... I hope you choke on your Bacardi and Coke/Look what you didn't take from me."

TWO OF RACHEL HUNTER'S EXES AT THE OPENING OF THE LONDON CLUB 'ROCK'

Shuffling love song *She's The One*, a cover of a World Party song released on their *Egyptology* album the previous year, came next ("If there's somebody calling me on/She's the one") then the nonsensical stomp of *Man Machine* ("How do you tell a joke when you can't laugh?/You know that you're the punchline/Baby, take a bath").

As with *Baby Girl Window*, the charming folky *These Dreams* written for his mum about Pete ("You never stopped loving his misfortunate lazy ways/All the memories that you should've had are a cabaret haze") seemed to be the last track, but two hidden songs followed. *Stand Your Ground* was literally Beach Boys-esque ("Stand your ground/The water's deep/Feel the sand/Beneath your feet") and the haunting, half-spoken *Stalker's Day Off* anticipated Eminem's *Stan*: "I've been hanging around/Just in case you fall in love with me... They don't understand you/Like I do."

Reviews and sales were strong, and second single *No Regrets* would chart at Number Four at the beginning of December. By the end of the year, Rob would be announced as the biggest selling album artist of 1998, having shifted almost two-and-a-half million copies of his solo albums, but success wasn't enough to ensure his sobriety. When Nicole finally walked out on him on Christmas Day, Rob went on another drinking binge and ended up at the Stakis Metropole Hotel in central London. After buying drinks for some strangers in the bar on Boxing Day morning he invited them back to his room to continue partying, but when they turned up he'd passed out on a sofa in the corridor. They took the opportunity to cover him in toothpaste and hair gel before taking photographs that ended up in the tabloids – hardly a fitting end to a spectacular year. "As far as I was concerned I was having a laugh and it was just high jinks," said Rob, "but I'm sad that they took advantage of my generosity."

His festive foolishness would soon be forgotten when the Brit Awards nominations were announced in late January. As expected by music industry analysts, Rob led the nominations with six nods: Best British Album for *I've Been Expecting You*, Best British Male Solo Artist, Best British Single (twice, for *Angels* and *Millennium*), and Best British Video for both *Let Me Entertain You* and *Millennium*.

Just days after his 25th birthday, Rob arrived at London Arena to perform *Millennium* at the Brits with a cast of 150 dancers; having smashed his head on his 'death slide' entrance during rehearsals, it went without a hitch. He left with three awards: Best British Male Solo Artist, Best British Single for *Angels* and Best British Video for *Millennium*. "This is all down to my mum," he said in his first acceptance speech of the night. "I know she'll be proud of me. I wouldn't be anywhere without her. I've made a lot of mistakes – so many I can't remember half of them – but my mum always believed in me."

Later, after Fatboy Slim accepted the Best British Dance Act award with a sheet of paper reading "Speechless", Rob held up a similar piece reading "Legless" before thanking David and Tim. Finally, he appeared genuinely lost for words when taking the Best British Single gong; "I have been planning, for three years, speeches when I win these awards. Obviously I didn't get one right..."

It was undoubtedly Rob's night, yet the presence of Nicole and her apparent new love Huey was enough to send him back on the booze. He tried not to react, telling tabloids "I've got three little ladies in my life now – my Brits. How many more do I need?" Yet he was soon shunning the mineral water on offer backstage for spirits, declaring "I've got an excuse to get drunk again and it feels great." His mother's calming influence would prevail ultimately, and Rob opted to go home to west London for a supper of baked beans-on-toast instead of attending after-show parties. Jan was modest about Rob's podium tribute, telling the press, "I've not done anything any mother would not do... He has done so well to address the problems he has had and it is all down to his own hard work. His next move will be the United States. He is confident he will make it over there and we are backing him 100 per cent."

With his reputation in the UK and Europe restored, Rob's management team prepared to do what Nigel Martin-Smith had dreamt of for Take That – take their charge to the US and repeat the success on an even grander scale. Import copies of his albums were already popular in America, and a US-only album, *The Ego Has Landed*, was being prepared, comprising the songs from *Life Thru A Lens* and *I've Been Expecting You* judged most likely to appeal to a Stateside audience. Ahead of the release, a string of small promo shows were arranged across the country. He'd made his US live debut before the Brits, playing to an invitation-only crowd in Los Angeles' Lucky Seven supper club. During a short set, he told the guests, "I'm nothing like my in-bred cousins from Manchester who like to spit on the audience," in reference to Oasis and their abortive attempts to impress the US. "I've always identified more with real classy singers such as Frank Sinatra and Dean Martin, and tonight you have made me feel a little closer to them."

He returned to America after the Brits, but the result wasn't what anyone was hoping for. The promo tour culminated in a show at the music showcase mecca of South By Southwest, a four-day industry festival held annually in Austin, Texas. Rob joined gravel-toned troubadour Tom Waits, psychedelic rockers The Flaming Lips and British folk queen Beth Orton and, although his European tour began the next day in Sweden, spent the night after his set on a Texas-sized bender. "He got completely shit-faced," said manager David. "I remember the next morning seeing his little face in the back of the limo, just not wanting to go to Stockholm... It was like sending a little boy off to school."

Rob had stayed up drinking all night with some local girls and "was all over the place" by the time the entourage reached the airport, his then-PA Gabby Chelmicka recalled. He was upgraded to first class and slept the entire flight but was still hungover and jetlagged when they arrived. "I turned up in Sweden and there was no way I could get on stage," said Rob. "No way I could present myself... My job is to get up on stage and be judged. And the judgements I was passing against myself at that time were terrible."

The Stockholm date was cancelled, and then the entire tour – a statement was released claiming that Rob was suffering from a "mystery virus" and unable to complete his current commitments. In truth, he flew from Sweden back to Jan's house to rest and recuperate. "This was a guy who was in the midst of his addictions and drinking, living in an illness and in deep denial," admitted David. "But the reason he was exhausted was because he was stuffing things up his nose and drinking too much."

March would continue to be a cruel month. Although the third single from *I've Been Expecting You*, *Strong*, followed *No Regrets* to Number Four, unfinished business from his previous life was to deal another blow to Rob's increasingly fragile ego. Having been

ordered by The High Court to pay Nigel Martin-Smith £90,000 in commission 18 months earlier, Rob had launched an appeal. He was now informed that his bid to overturn the ruling had failed, and was re-ordered to pay the £90,000 plus legal costs, interest, VAT, damages and additional commission payments adding to up to around £1million.

IE's statement was dismissive of the ruling – "Robbie is concentrating on the hugely successful career he has built up since his split with Nigel Martin-Smith and he has left his lawyers to deal with this tedious case" – even though £1million was still a considerable sum to their client. The man himself responded to the press with V-signs from the windows of his home. Nigel's final words were more contemplative than crowing: "I really was very fond of Robbie, but he's not the same lad that I took off the dole and made into a star all those years ago. Robbie has had two attempts at trying to persuade a court of law that I acted badly towards him. He has now failed twice. My only hope is that, in time, Robbie will come to see things as they actually were, not as his mother has chosen to see them."

Having settled Tim Abbott's £1.2million claim out of court the previous year for an undisclosed fee, it would be another year before he was free of legal wrangles with ex-managers – he eventually agreed to pay Kevin Kinsella "a substantial sum" plus costs, adding up to almost half a million pounds, in August 2000 – but other cases awaited.

In April 1999, folk singer Loudon Wainwright III announced his intention to sue Rob and Guy Chambers for copyright infringement of his song *I Am The Way (New York Town)* off his 1973 album *Attempted Moustache*. *I've Been Expecting You*'s *Jesus In A Camper Van* featured the lines "Even the son of God/Gets it hard sometimes/Especially when he goes round/Saying I am the way". Loudon claimed they were a direct infringement of his words, "Every son of God gets a little hard work sometimes/Especially when he goes around saying he's the way," based on the 1961 song *New York Way* by cult folk musician Woody Guthrie. Court records would reveal that EMI had approached Loudon's publishers, New York-based Ludlow Music Inc, in the summer before Rob's album was released to ask permission to use the lyrics. Ludlow wanted 50 per cent of the copyright fees or the removal of all references, which EMI refused, offering instead 25 per cent and crediting Loudon with co-writing the track. By May, Woody's estate had also launched a lawsuit and was seeking to prevent the sale of the offending album and recoup millions in damages.

It would be another horrendously expensive and long-drawn-out legal dispute. In October 2000, a judge ruled that Ludlow, who owned the rights to both Loudon's "parody" and Woody's original, were entitled to "substantial... exemplary" damages from Rob, Guy, EMI Music Publishing and BMG Music Publishing (who shared the copyright) because "in my view, the extent of the copying is substantial, although not by much". On appeal, a different judge ruled in February 2002 that EMI's offer of 25 per cent was acceptable, amounting to a payment to Ludlow of around £50,000, and that additional damages were unnecessary because it was a minor infringement in a song without "staying power"; legal fees were expected to cost another quarter of a million pounds. He ordered that future pressings of *I've Been Expecting You* must remove the track entirely (it was replaced with *It's Only Us*, the double a-side from the November 1999 Number One single *She's The One*) adding that he had "grave doubts as to who has actually won this case". Rob's accountants would surely agree.

ROB'S DRINK AND DRUG ADDICTIONS HAD HAUNTED HIM FOR YEARS.

chapter 8

BETTER
MAN?

THE EGO HAS LANDED WAS RELEASED IN THE US ON THE CAPITOL LABEL in May 1999. It comprised six tracks from *Life Thru A Lens* – the post-*Freedom* singles (less *South Of The Border*) plus *Killing Me* and *One Of God's Better People* – and eight from *I've Been Expecting You* – the four singles plus *Win Some, Lose Some, Jesus in a Camper Van, Man Machine*, and *Karma Killer*. (Later versions would substitute *Jesus In A Camper Van* with *Phoenix From The Flames*.) In contrast to the arrogant name – a former working title for *Life Thru A Lens* – the cover art showed only Rob's eyes and forehead shyly emerging from a turtle-neck jumper, a decidedly un-Robbie pose.

Reviews were positive: "Robbie Williams served his time as the bad-apple boy in Take That [and his] US solo debut... proves that he's one teen idol who knows how to make a lovably lurid showbiz spectacle of himself," wrote America's most revered music magazine, *Rolling Stone*. "*The Ego Has Landed* is smartly crafted, hormonally charged, utterly content-free boy-preen that even grown-ups can flip for."

In support of the record, Rob returned to North America for another round of promotional duties. He appeared at the same-sized venues he'd played on his first solo tour of the UK, and MTV News spent a weekend with him for their *Next Big Thing* program; even in virgin territory old anxieties surfaced. When quizzed about *Karma Killer*, Rob revealed "The American record company didn't want that on the album, but I insisted that it went on. That song's a glorious gloating in my success... I'm spreading the word to America about what a bastard [Nigel Martin-Smith] is."

With the glowing *Rolling Stone* review under his belt, a prestigious guest spot on cult chat show *The Late Show With David Letterman* was also arranged, a coup for such an unknown artist. After a performance of his first US single, *Millennium*, a visibly nervous Rob took a seat and told the host how honoured he was to be there before stumbling over a string of throwaway gags that were somehow lost in translation. When a picture of Rob in Take That was shown, he quipped, "That's not me, that's my brother" – but neither David nor the audience knew who he was, or that this was another joke. Although the live shows were a success – he sold out New York's hip Bowery Ballroom – and US magazine *Entertainment Weekly* included him in their 'It List' of the world's hottest 100 talents (citing him as a "supernova in his native England"), *Millennium* wasn't a hit and the album was as slow to sell in the States as it had been in the UK.

Back home in the UK, Rob had to prepare for his biggest headline gig to date at the end of August. Although the Slane Castle show in County Meath, Ireland would feature six support acts, all 80,000 tickets had been sold before they had even been announced so, unlike at Glastonbury, everyone would be there just to see him. Rob had played the venue the previous summer in support of The Verve, then the biggest-sellers of the year with their third album, *Urban Hymns*, so he knew what to expect – if anything, this made the experience all the more terrifying.

CHAPTER OPENER: PERFORMING AT THE FESTIVALBAR ARENA IN MILAN

RIGHT: THE SLANE CASTLE SHOW SOLD OUT BEFORE ANY ACT – OTHER THAN ROB – HAD BEEN ANNOUNCED

Just weeks before the show, exhausted from his promotional workload and daunted by the size of the Slane crowd awaiting him, he almost suffered a breakdown. "What stopped me from really going mad was a week I spent in Los Angeles," he later revealed. "Basically, I flew out there thinking that I didn't want to carry on any more, but I came back believing this is actually the best job in the world." Rob was believed to have taken a week of stress-counselling from a leading LA psychiatrist to help him cope. He was also advised that owning a pet might help him handle his loneliness, so he bought two Rhodesian Ridgebacks: "They are both puppies at the moment, but are built like lions."

For the 80,000-strong crowd, Slane '99 was an undoubted success. For Rob, it was a nightmare; moments before going onstage he was gripped by a panic attack. He admitted afterwards, "It was the biggest event I've ever done but I was so unhappy and so scared. It's the feeling of realising that no matter how successful you are, it doesn't make you a whole person... I realise that was a fabulous night [but] I went through it as if I wasn't there." Questioning his entire career, he talked about returning to the theatre. "I just thought, 'I don't want to do this any more'. I wanted to act. I wanted to give up music and tread the boards."

To make matters worse, Rob's old allies were now turning against him. Early in their acquaintance Noel Gallagher had offered to write Rob a song; in February 2000 he revoked their friendship. In an interview to promote Oasis' fourth album, *Standing On The Shoulder Of Giants*, Noel claimed "I've never been his friend. He was Liam's friend. Liam used to invite him to the gigs and stuff like that. I've been in dressing rooms with him, I've had conversations with him, but I wouldn't even consider him to be a friend of mine. Why? Because he was in Take That! He's a fat dancer from Take That. Somebody who danced for a living. Stick to what you're good at, that's what I always say." Liam added, "We were never friends anyway. We might say a polite hello, that's it... I think Robbie's music's rubbish but he's better than that other twat he was in a band with."

(Liam had previously called him "tubby-arsed Williams" and when Oasis were asked to record a version of *Angels* for BBC Radio 1 Noel refused, saying Liam would have to "sing it with 50 meat pies in his mouth." In response, Rob said during an interview, "I knew I could write poetry but I also knew I only knew three chords. And those three chords can't last forever... unless you're Oasis.")

Rob's response to the "fat dancer" jibe was swift. Within days he sent a £100 funeral wreath of white roses and lilies to Noel via *The Sun*'s showbiz desk, with a note reading, "To Noel Gallagher, RIP. Heard your latest album, with deepest sympathy, Robbie Williams." (He had bought a bootleg of the album in London's Camden Market and declared, "Noel's run out of other people's ideas.") Infuriated by the slur on his new record Liam resorted to physical threats, telling *The Big Breakfast*, "It's the best fucking album out this year, better than anything Fatty will ever do... You can tell that cunt if I ever see him in a club in London – I'm gonna break his fucking nose. He'll be needing wreaths on *his* door. Rest in peace!" With Oasis on tour in Japan, Rob replied airily, "Oh, he's going to beat me up, is he? I'm just not angry enough to hit him – it's not my career going down the drain. But if he hits me I suppose I'll have to defend myself."

At the 2000 Brit Awards, he laid down a formal challenge to Liam. Taking home the

Best Single and Best Video trophies for *She's The One* in a year when Oasis weren't even nominated, Rob suggested "We'll get in the ring and we'll have a fight and you can watch it on TV – what do you think about that? Would anybody like to see me fight Liam? Would you pay to come and see it?" He offered to wager £100,000 on the outcome, asking "Are you going to do it or are you going to pussy out, you fucking wimp?" (The fight almost overshadowed the fact that with nine Brits to his credit now – four from his time in Take That – Rob was now the most successful artist in Brits history.)

Bookies William Hill soon revealed their odds – "Robbie has a weight advantage and would be 1/2 favourite to see off Liam" – while a variety of promoters announced they would be willing to stage the bout, but the Oasis camp remained atypically quiet. The words of an "unnamed source" within the band sounded like a climb-down from the younger Gallagher: "The whole thing is pathetic. All these people, including newspapers, Robbie himself and boxing promoters seem to be getting mileage out of violence. It's sick. ... Whatever Liam said in the first place was said in jest. He never wanted this to become an issue." Back in the UK from Japan, Noel attempted to end the feud, albeit with a barb: "I doubt Robbie has got a hundred grand... [but] it's all forgotten now."

By April, the real source of the animosity would be hinted at in the tabloids: Nicole Appleton. Although Liam was still married to Patsy Kensit, a "friendship" with Rob's erstwhile fiancée was reported before the couple split and divorced. In July, all was revealed in the tabloids – hours before Oasis' sold-out Wembley Stadium show, Liam and Nicole were snapped kissing in public. "Robbie thinks her romance with the man he regards as his arch enemy is the ultimate betrayal," revealed "a pal of Nicole's". "Nicole's big problem is that Robbie is so annoyed. He's very protective of her."

(Liam was no stranger to musical love triangles – the Oasis-Blur feud was said to stem from Damon Albarn bedding Liam's then girlfriend, sometime-singer Lisa Moorish, during the heady days of Britpop. Lisa later gave birth to Liam's lookalike daughter, Molly – conceived a week after he married Patsy.)

Rob soon had a new woman in his life too. Days after the paparazzi caught Nicole and Liam together, they would snap Rob leaving his new Notting Hill home in the company of Spice Girl-turned-solo singer Geri Halliwell. Introduced through EMI, whose label Chrysalis they were both signed to, the pair were next seen enjoying a £10,000-a-week St Tropez holiday together, splashing around in (not-so) private pools and clinging onto each other during moped rides through the countryside of southern France. With Rob's third album due for release in a few weeks and Geri's first autobiography, *If Only*, just published in paperback, it was quickly dismissed as another elaborate Halliwell publicity stunt, yet behind the tabloid stories a strong friendship was forming.

Throughout his problems with addiction and ongoing lack of success with women (he announced in June 2000: "I've never been in love. Yeah, I was engaged, but in this crazy mixed-up world of showbiz, that doesn't mean anything really, does it?"), Rob had turned to his friends for support when he felt unable to approach his family. Not all his friendships would survive his success. Rob recalled ringing his old school mate Lee Hancock after finding fame with Take That and asking to come round. "He said, 'Well, I need to clean the house and put my suit on.' And then he was all embarrassed because his house was a mess. And it made me really sad. Because he just wouldn't have bothered in the old days." Instead, Rob hooked up with another local lad and their relationship would weather both his success and his failings.

Jan met Eileen Wilkes on holiday in Majorca in the mid '80s and the pair introduced their sons, Rob and Jonathan. Back in Stoke-on-Trent they stayed in touch and the boys became like brothers – appearing together on stage for the first time in the chorus of *Hans Christian Anderson*. As the older Rob left home to become part of Take That, Jonathan failed in his attempts to become a footballer for Everton FC (he was deemed too small to succeed) and, after an early spate of binge-drinking and comfort-eating, discovered a talent for singing. Thanks to his dad's negotiating nous, the 17-year-old Jonathan became the youngest-ever headliner in Blackpool, at the Pleasure Beach's Star Bar. After fulfilling a three-year contract, during which time his revue show *Jonathan Wilkes and the Space Girls* became a big local success, Jonathan was offered a presenting job on the fledgling digital TV channel BBC Choice. He jumped at the opportunity and took Rob up on his offer to stay at his Notting Hill home until he found himself a place of his own; "I ended up staying four years." With his own rebellious phase long since over, Jonathan "became the big brother, the one looking out for Rob." He would stay sober to watch over his drunken friend and beg people at parties to not give his famous flatmate drugs. "When Rob drinks he turns into someone that I don't know," explained Jonathan, "a slag; aggressive, rude. He hasn't got any sense of humour, no appreciation of life."

Their closeness – "We need each other... if he had his way he'd have me with him 24 hours a day" – led to a rebirth of interest in the gay rumours that had surrounded Rob ever since the first days of Take That. Not that Rob cared. In one interview from 2000 he announced, "All these people you hear that I've been sleeping with are all men... I am gay anyway, but don't tell anyone," before a friend hastily pointed out that he was only joking. Another time, when pressed by an inquisitive Australian journalist, he replied, "I tried being gay but it wasn't for me. If I could take a gay pill right now I would. But I'm just not." Mel B from the Spice Girls told a TV audience "He prefers men", but Rob's on-stage retort "I was in Take That. I've also been in a couple of the Spice Girls..." would imply that she was perhaps trying to protect a dumped Mel C's pride. Ditto Liam's sneering comments at the *Q* magazine awards, when he said "He understands the letter Q... for queer." Rob's old manager Kevin Kinsella has also said "I think he's totally gay," based on his extremely addled behaviour during their six-month working relationship.

Like the lyric "Am I straight or gay?" from *Old Before I Die*, a mock-rapped line from his new album – "Press be asking do I care for sodomy/I don't know, yeah, probably" from *Kids* – would pique the public's interest in his sexuality yet further, yet all the proof Rob can possibly offer to being heterosexual is a string of beautiful girlfriends and Jonathan's recent marriage.

Sing When You're Winning was released at the end of August 2000, a full year after Rob almost quit the business. A less sound-a-like album than the previous two, it was the most wholly Robbie record yet and a tribute to his years in and out of therapy; the lyrics weren't casting blame but finding salvation from within. Anthemic opener *Let Love Be Your Energy* was an ode to positivity ("If you're willing to change the world/Let love be

your energy"), *Better Man,* a John Lennon-inspired ballad about self-improvement ("As my soul heals the shame/I will grow through this pain"). Lead single *Rock DJ* was, by contrast, a strictly disco track, with insights into the seedier side of the music industry ("Music for your masses/Give no head, no backstage passes") while *Supreme,* based around a credited copy of Gloria Gaynor's classic *I Will Survive,* was a humorous look at the dating game: "All the best women are married/All the handsome men are gay." *Kids,* a duet with Kylie Minogue, was an anti-love song about their unsuitability for one another and production line pop (Rob: "You can't just up and leave me/I'm a singer in a band"; Kylie: "Well I like drummers, baby/You're not my bag") with a sarcastic rap at the end ("Single-handedly raising the economy/Ain't no chance of the record company dropping me...").

The low-key *If It's Hurtin' You* was written about the split with Nicole ("I'm not a gigolo/That's what I want you to know") while the jangly *Singing For The Lonely* contemplated the two sides to Rob's personality, "The hooligan half of me... the other lives for love". *Love Calling Earth* was a '60s sounding mediation on his lack of luck with ladies ("How do I learn/To give love and be loved in return?"), *Knutsford City Limits* a jokey reference to Tina Turner and the Macc Lads ("London's got its gimmicks/And New York's had its minute/But Knutsford city limits/I'll never change") that could have sat comfortably on *Life Thru A Lens.* The insistent, crunchy *Forever Texas* offered a conversation with a potential new love ("Everybody wants to know how I'm hung/You can read it in the papers"), while the strings-laden *By All Means Necessary* was the bitterest moment on the record, a withering assessment of a celebrity groupie: "It's not a BAFTA you're after/You want a million dollar lay". The folky last track *The Road To Mandalay* ("This sombre song would drain the sun") ended the album with an oddly maudlin singalong.

Sing When You're Winning would follow *Rock DJ* to Number One on the first week of release, and another extensive European tour was undertaken in support of the album. As documented in the film *Nobody Someday,* The Sermon on the Mount tour was difficult, with a freshly-sober Rob forced to face his demons without the aid of drink and drugs. With co-manager David acting as his on-tour AA sponsor and bodyguards to help him resist temptation, Rob asked that the crew abstain in his presence and he spent most of his down-time drinking mineral water and playing card games.

As the tour went on, he slowly overcame his doubts about his career. Initially, he said "I actually had contempt for my audience for coming to see someone so shit..." By the end, he admitted, "All those people out there enjoyed themselves tonight, and I did too."

Not only had Rob coped with his inner demons, he'd also survived an attack from an outsider. In Stuttgart's Schleyerhalle stadium in February 2001, a psychotic fan gained access to the stage and pushed him off, face-forwards into the security pit. As the crowd gasped and the band stopped dead, the assailant was apprehended and Rob was helped back on stage. "Is everybody OK?" he asked, visibly shaken. "Well so am I, and I'm not going to let any fucker get on stage and stop you having a good time." He completed the set, even though he would later tell the camera crew he was "genuinely scared" by the assault. As David proudly noted, "Old Robbie would have been furious and run away... it was a turning point. The boy became a man."

chapter 9

SOMETHIN'
STUPID

THROUGHOUT GUY'S MUSICAL FLIRTATIONS WITH ROCK, EASY LISTENING, pop and folk on the albums, dad Pete's record collection of crooners and their swing classics remained a constant influence over Rob's singing style. Although his memories of the first record he ever bought waver depending on who asks him – he's variously claimed it was Pink Floyd's 1979 concept album *The Wall*, The Sugarhill Gang's innovative *Rapper's Delight* from the same year or a Glenn Miller big band LP – the early presence of Frank Sinatra and his Rat Pack in Rob's life was definite. As well as owning the records, Pete included swing classics in his stage performances and his young mimic son soon learnt to imitate them, note-perfect. Former teen idol Bobby Darin's jazzy version of murder ballad *Mack The Knife* became his party-piece, delivered at karaoke nights and family gatherings with his father's affected mid-Atlantic singing accent.

Rob remembers Sundays spent enthralled by his dad's cherished records, teaching himself their slang and style. "I would go into the front room and put on records. It would always be Nat King Cole, Sammy Davis Jnr, Dean Martin, Frank Sinatra, Sarah Vaughan and Ella Fitzgerald" – part of his pre-show preparation, along with the "Elvis ritual" Serenity Prayer, is to superstitiously kiss framed images of his idols Frank, Dino and Sammy (and boxer Muhammad Ali). Early in his solo career he paid a small tribute on the b-side of *Lazy Days* with a cover of Ella Fitzgerald's *Ev'ry Time We Say Goodbye* – the same song he'd sung on leaving school – but his new stamping ground, the stadium circuit, was hardly conducive to any live appreciations.

In early 2001, the big screen version of comic novel *Bridget Jones's Diary* was in post-production and the soundtrack was being assembled. Early previews of the movie featured original versions of songs that would be covered for the finished product, including The Weather Girls' *It's Raining Men* and Rodgers and Hart's musical standard *Have You Met Miss Jones?*; Geri Halliwell would provide a new Hi-NRG version of the former, while co-screenwriter Richard Curtis suggested Rob for an authentic-sounding swing version of the latter. With the Sermon On The Mount tour finally out of the way and the trauma of the on-stage attack behind him, he agreed, eventually contributing a second track, the newly-written Williams-Chambers ballad *Not Of This World*, too. As the finished *Bridget Jones's Diary* became an international hit, Rob was asked to record a version of Queen's *We Are The Champions* for the soundtrack of forthcoming Arthurian comedy *A Knight's Tale*. In LA to film a video for the track, he secured a spot on the top-rated chat show in America, *The Tonight Show with Jay Leno*, to perform *Have You Met Miss Jones?* The appearance wasn't a repeat of his awkward David Letterman experience, and the thrill of performing the swing classic live reawakened his love of the genre.

Once back in the UK, Rob presented his idea to managers Tim and David: "Look guys, why don't we do a swing album for Christmas?" A fourth album wasn't even scheduled yet, and Rob had originally planned to take the year off to recharge, but his enthusiasm

CHAPTER OPENER: EURO STAR – PERFORMING IN CANNES AT THE NRJ MUSIC AWARDS...

RIGHT: ...AND IN BARCELONA AT THE MTV EUROPE MUSIC AWARDS

persuaded Tim and David to take the idea to EMI. It's common practise for artists to deliver a live or Greatest Hits record to fulfil contractual obligations and move to a new label, and EMI were worried that the proposed album sounded like a novelty release to allow Rob to complete his four-album deal with them – they didn't think it would sell. Eventually EMI relented and, after the remaining UK and Irish live dates of the Weddings, Bar Mitzvahs, Stadiums tour were played out, studio time was booked in LA at the Capitol Studios where Frank, Dino and Sammy had often recorded.

Even if his zeal for live performing had returned, Rob was becoming increasingly weary of his alter-ego – "I'm really bored with Robbie... I'm just going to kill him off. I'm everywhere. It must be really boring for people" – and the swing project was just what he needed, a chance to try something new and bring his lifelong passion into his day-job.

Authenticity was the key to the sessions . As well as the studio, EMI had arranged for the orchestra to be made up of the best jazz musicians around, including some who had backed the Rat Pack's own recordings. It was a dream come true for Rob: "I'm singing my favourite songs with a full orchestra, and getting paid for it." At the end of a successful take he told the amassed musicians, Guy and his managers, "I've found my spiritual home." Like EMI, Rob didn't really expect the album to be a huge hit back home, but that wasn't why he was doing it. "I'd been thinking, 'Why did I get into this game in the first place?' And it was just for those... hours [in the Capitol Studio]." It was, he would tell the press, "the most fun I have ever had recording. My only complaint is that my fingers are sore from clicking them – I'm suffering from 'swing finger' – and my jaw muscles are aching from pulling my new 'jazz face'."

For variety, and added appeal if the swing treatment failed to attract the usual Robbie Williams fanbase, Rob and Guy decided to include a series of duets on the record. Jonathan Wilkes would get his biggest break to date on the appropriately chosen Frank and Sammy song *Me and My Shadow*; British *Little Voice* actress and singer Jane Horrocks would sing on Bobby Darin's *Things* (returning the favour Rob did by appearing on her 2000 album *The Further Adventures of Little Voice*, singing Ella's smoky standard *That Old Black Magic*); and US comic performer Jon Lovitz would appear on the bitchy Cole Porter classic *Well, Did You Evah?*. LA-dwelling Brit actor Rupert Everett would share the vocal on George and Ira Gershwin's *They Can't Take That Away From Me* and Nicole Kidman, on the cusp of superstardom after her split from Tom Cruise and stellar turn in Baz Luhrmann's *Moulin Rouge*, would pair up with Rob on Frank's *Somethin' Stupid*. (Rob persuaded Nicole to take part by sending her a note reading simply, "Will you be Nancy to my Frank?" and, admitting herself to be "a terrible businesswoman", she agreed. "The arse just fell out of my world for a couple of days," said Rob. "I thought: 'How am I supposed to get through this and not look like an idiot – or try to lick her face?' [but] we got on really well. Nicole has a beautiful voice and I was amazed how well we worked together." Their first meeting was at the Capitol Studios and, while both were nervous, the song was completed in under an hour.) Perhaps most remarkably of all, impressed by his enthusiasm in the studio, Rob's backing musicians contacted the Sinatra estate and arranged for him to share vocals with the deceased icon on a digitally reworked version of *It Was A Very Good Year*.

With the record complete and being readied for the Christmas market – the cover image was styled with Rob in a '60s-style shirt and tie with side-parted, slicked-back hair, beneath the same vintage Capitol logo that had graced Frank's albums – a one-off live show was arranged to air the material, rather than attempt to take it on tour. London's prestigious Royal Albert Hall, a venue Rob had already played successfully as a solo artist, was chosen as the location. Having told MTV in his first US interview that he wanted to "get to the point where I'm doing shows where I sing a song and then I tell jokes and tell a story and feel as comfortable as [the Rat Pack] looked on the stage, how they phrased things and the banter they had going," Rob called in a favour from future *Love Actually* writer-director Richard Curtis and enlisted his comedy skills to help pen his between-song quips and the risqué material that compére Rupert Everett would deliver. Along with Rupert, Jane, Jon and Jonathan would all appear to reprise their duets – too nervous to sing live, Nicole would attend but not perform.

Ahead of the big night on 10 October, a warm-up was held at Ronnie Scott's Jazz Club in Soho; "I battered 'em," said Rob of the ecstatic reaction from the 100 or so people making up the crowd. Although his nerves would re-appear before going on stage at the Royal Albert Hall, the sheer panic that had gripped him ahead of earlier stadium shows was thankfully absent and with Jonathan's parents and Jan in the audience (despite Pete being the inspiration for the evening, he wasn't invited, as he and Rob weren't currently on speaking terms) his confidence soon returned.

"Here he is, the most paranoid man in showbusiness, straight from a very expensive rehab centre... to sing the songs he was born to sing" quipped Rupert as Rob made his entrance by sliding down a fireman's pole and stomping across a set of kettle drums in front of the formally-attired 3,500 fans who had paid between £100 and £20,000 for a ticket and celebrity guests including Nicole, who sat with *The Hours* director-to-be Stephen Daldry. "It's a very special night for me," Rob announced. "A night that I'm going to pay tribute to the coolest men that ever lived – Mr Sammy Davis Jnr, Mr Dean Martin, Mr Frank Sinatra... and [*Popstars* winner] Danny out of Hear'Say." As he pretended to chat up his 20-strong female troupe ("Robbie says take your skirts off. Robbie says go back to the Ritz where I'm staying, go straight to suite 811 and wait for me buck-naked...") and Rupert delivered a string of obscene asides ("Despite whatever sexual orientation you came in the building with, would you get down on all fours and be royally shagged by Robbie Williams?"), many of which wouldn't survive the TV edit, the 58-piece orchestra delivered the half-century-old hits in pristine condition. The show opened with *Have You Met Miss Jones?* and ended, as any Frank Sinatra tribute should, with *My Way*; *Somethin' Stupid* was dropped from the set when Nicole politely declined to sing but versions of *Let's Face The Music And Dance* ("Let's get buck-naked and fucked-up on drugs..." trilled Rob, by way of an intro) and *The Lady Is A Tramp* ("Ladies and gentlemen, this next song is dedicated to my last three girlfriends") ably filled the gap.

Nat King Cole's *Straighten Up And Fly Right* was dedicated to Jan ("Mum, this is your son singing – I love you") and *Me And My Shadow* with its unsubtly re-worded lyrics delivered the self-deprecating highlight of the show. "We're closer than smog is to all of LA/We're closer than Ricky [Martin] to confessing he's gay..." sang Rob before a skit towards the end: "Can we do that again?" "No, I'm too tired" "I won't tell everybody that you're gay..." The cinematic new Williams-Chambers song *I Will Talk And Hollywood Will Listen* fell midway through the set ("Kevin Spacey would call on the phone... Cameron Diaz, give me a sign... Mr Spielberg, look just what you're missing"), momentarily returning Rob's voice to its usual, higher singing range. Before *My Way*, Rob prefaced a (half-)live version of *It Was A Very Good Year* with the admission that the experience "made me cry"; Frank then appeared on giant video screens to deliver his verses.

As could be expected for such an atypically Robbie evening, the critical response was mixed – "A good night, Robbie, but don't give up your day job"; "A masterstroke, a metamorphosis from former boy-band rock-boy to sophisticated performer"; "The lavish nature of the one-off event... could not disguise the essential emptiness of Williams' unspectacular interpretations"; "Full marks to Robbie Williams for being brave enough to be different" – but the weekend before the accompanying album was finally released BBC One screened the show on TV. It drew 7.3 million viewers to BBC – but more than 130 complaints were received, most relating to Rupert's "royally shagged" line. Yet even with the live show and TV broadcast a success, the album itself remained an unknown quantity. Was the UK really ready to swing with Robbie Williams?

The answer was a resounding yes. *Swing When You're Winning* went straight to Number One and sold 300,000 copies in its first week; by the end of the year it had shifted well over a million units, making it the second-biggest selling record of 2001 behind Dido's *No Angel*. *Somethin' Stupid* was selected as the single, and a Christmassy video shot with Rob and Nicole frolicking in a mocked-up ski chalet in matching jumpers. Bookies William Hill initially put their chances of Christmas Number One success as only 12/1, tipping Kate Winslet's *If Only*, taken from the soundtrack to the animated *Christmas Carol: The Movie*, to win the race at 7/2. But aided by incessant press speculation about a real-life romance between the couple – after Nicole appeared on the *Parkinson* chat show with *Moulin Rouge* co-star Ewan McGregor she sped back to her hotel, The Dorchester, and Rob arrived five minutes later, staying until 3am – it went to the top of the charts and, like the album, stayed there over the Christmas period.

When Rob next played in Sydney, Nicole watched the show from the wings and the two met up at the after-show party and her home in the exclusive Darling Point district, but it would be a year before he revealed what had actually happened between them. Debuting tracks from his fifth album before an invited audience of fans, he introduced *How Peculiar* as "a song about a certain person who shall remain nameless. Every time I was near her I felt like I was a seven-year-old and that I had nothing to say. Fortunately she found me attractive so I wrote this song to say 'I think you're ace'. In the end I didn't know what to say, so I just got my penis out." He added, "Have you ever been really obsessed with someone, to the point where you can't eat or drink, to the point where you can't think about anything but that person?" The lyrics included the lines: "Need for you to love me so much/Jesus, what am I going to do with this crush/So get the old fella and whack it up against her tush... Bend your long legs against the sofa in the Dorchester."

After the rendition, he dispensed with further euphemisms:

"Needless to say, I slept with her."

chapter 10

SOMETHING
BEAUTIFUL

ROB WOULD CONTINUE HIS BRITS WINNING STREAK AT THE 2001 CEREMONY on 26 February – he won all three categories he was nominated in, starting with Best British Male Solo Artist. The award was presented by Geri Halliwell, resplendent in her post-yoga slimness and a micro-miniskirt. "I'll give you a clue," she said as she opened the envelope. "He's very male, he's very healthy, he's a talented artist, he's got the biggest heart and, wait for it, according to the press he's been giving me one. So let me return the favour by giving him one – my very dear friend, Mr Robert Williams!" Rob would go on to take the trophies for Best British Video and Best British Single for *Rock DJ* – taking his solo tally of Brits to eight – after which he, Geri and Jonathan Wilkes went back to his house to celebrate by drinking tea and playing card games.

"We just sat around playing *Uno* and chatted," said Jonathan later, on the promotional trail for his single *Just Another Day* (which would chart at a disappointing Number 24). "We're all normal people and are all very similar... Geri's only little, but she's become our big sister." She was more than just a big sister to Rob – he described her as his "guardian angel" when she accompanied him to Alcoholics Anonymous meetings to help his ongoing sobriety.

In her autobiographies, *If Only* and *Just For The Record*, Geri admitted to issues with food throughout her life. At her lowest point, she endured binge and purge regimes that even saw her scavenge food from dustbins in hunger. While never addicted to drink or drugs, her new-found control over her body image – attributed to a sugar-free diet and hours of intensive yoga – made her the ideal aid and inspiration to Rob during his own battles. He would repay her selflessness on his summer single, a double a-side featuring *The Road To Mandalay* and *Eternity*, a platonic love song written especially for her: "You were there for summer dreaming/And you are a friend indeed/And I hope you find your freedom/Eventually." The single was Number One for three weeks in July, but within months their special friendship was in tatters.

On 18 November, *The Sunday Times* published an interview by music journalist Adrian Deevoy in which Rob came clean about his relationship with Geri. "She turned into a demonic little girl playing with dolls and a tea set," he said. "She started speaking like a psychotic child and she developed this possessed look in her eye. It was genuinely scaring me. It was around that time I realised our friendship wasn't what I thought it was... I'd be lying if I said I [missed her]." He also admitted that the pair had slept together, but added "I don't think we found each other physically attractive. It wasn't really a sex thing."

Although he would later retract the sex confession, claim he was misquoted and attempt to apologise to Geri during a three-hour phone call, their friendship would never recover. All footage of her would subsequently be cut from the film *Nobody Someday* which documented much of Rob's 2001, and when the two were booked to appear on the Christmas edition of chat show *Parkinson* Rob insisted on recording his performance in

CHAPTER OPENER: ADMIRING THE VIEW DURING THE 'FASHION ROCKS' SHOW AT THE ROYAL ALBERT HALL IN OCTOBER 2003

RIGHT: ROB CELEBRATES SIGNING A NEW FOUR-ALBUM, "MULTI-PLATFORM" DEAL WITH EMI ESTIMATED TO BE WORTH £80 MILLION

the afternoon before the main taping so as to avoid Geri (and her wrath). The broadcast show was edited to imply Geri was watching Rob live; after the performance, when asked by the host if she likes him, she replied, "Yes. Yes, I love him." Most tellingly of all, *Eternity*, too contemporary to have found a home on *Swing When You're Winning*, would be notable by its absence from Rob's next album.

Rob was finding fame useless in assuaging the feelings of worthlessness that, sober, he was now forced to confront. He admitted after the Brits that he didn't often "feel worthy enough to be in [the] company" of his supposed peers Sir Elton John (he was knighted at the end of 1998) and Bono from U2 – "If I speak to them for too long then they're going to know I'm a charlatan" – and that he felt like a prisoner in own home. "When I go outside and around Notting Hill there are people there looking at me and following me," he told a photographer. "What would you say if I told you that I sit inside crying because I don't know what to do?"

During the *Swing* sessions in LA, Rob came to appreciate the benefits of having not yet made a name for himself in America. "He's able to live a normal life [there]," said manager Tim. "He can walk out the door, go down the street and not be hassled." In a city where Oscar-winners can shop unmolested and recovery, self-improvement and healthy-living is almost as big an industry as showbusiness, Rob realised his spiritual home wasn't just the Capitol Studios, but Los Angeles itself.

His first home there was a house rented from actor Dan Ackroyd on Mulholland Drive in Beverly Hills. Before too long Rob had hooked up with LA's thriving ex-pat community of British actors and musicians – ordaining himself as a priest on the Internet with the Universal Ministries And Universal Life Church in order to marry Cult bassist Billy Morrison to girlfriend Jennifer Holliday. Rob also seemingly found himself an unlikely new girlfriend, Kiwi swimsuit model/actress Rachel Hunter, Rod Stewart's second ex-wife. Almost five years his senior, Rachel could empathise with Rob's problems having spent years in therapy to address feelings of guilt at leaving Rod "to find herself". "She feels genuinely content with him and is hoping the romance will be long-term," a "friend" confided to the tabloids. Doorstepped leaving an AA meeting, Rob refuted the claims: "Rachel and I are definitely not an item. We are not seeing each other and are not together in any way." They were, however, both seen proudly sporting new tattoos.

Since acquiring the Celtic cross atop his right thigh towards the end of his time in Take That, Rob had covered much of his skin in body art. A large, seemingly abstract design on his left shoulder is in fact a symbolic Maori verse, adapted by Jan: "It's a prayer, protecting me from myself." On the other shoulder Rob has the face of a lion with a banner beneath reading "Born To Be Mild", and above it the words of his AA mantra: "Elvis, Grant Me Serenity". On his wrists, he has the name of his maternal granddad – "Jack" and "Farrell" – and higher up the words "I LOVE U" and "MOTHER" rendered in ornate"calligraphy down both arms. He added the letter "B' behind his left ear in memory of his Nan, Betty, who died in 1998, and an old-style religious illustration on his inner right arm. At the base of his spine he has a fully annotated score of the chorus from The Beatles' *All You Need Is Love* and around his neck the French words "CHACUN À SON GOUT" ("Everybody to his own taste"). His left wrist bears the digits "1023", deciphered

were suitably irreverent: "Sent the villains to Hades/A hit with the ladies/A stallion in the sack... So charismatic, willing, automatic/Never prematurely shooting his load."

By the summer he was back in the UK, preparing for what would be his biggest ever live shows. Three nights at the 125,000-capacity venue of Knebworth Park had been announced as the only UK dates on his world tour. Oasis had played two consecutive nights at Knebworth in 1996 at the height of their fame; by adding a third, Rob smashed their record and delivered another blow to the Gallagher's egos. Tickets sold out in hours nine months before the shows and, apart from traffic problems that left hundreds of fans stranded in jams miles from the site, the weekend was a triumph. "I'm the happiest man on the planet," Rob told the throng, before welcoming a special guest onstage. When Mark Owen won a celebrity version of *Big Brother* the year before, he returned to the spotlight and signed a new recording contract; after the pair hugged, they delivered Rob's preferred rock version of *Back For Good* to an ecstatic reaction. Rob even strummed a few bars of *Wonderwall* during the final show, adding drily, "This is the only time you'll hear that song on a third night at Knebworth."

After Knebworth came another boost to his career; *Finding Nemo*, now the most successful animated movie of all time, used his version of *Beyond The Sea* over the end titles, bringing him to the notice of an enormous global audience. Also impressed by his swing prowess – not least his version of *Well, Did You Evah?* – producers of a new Cole Porter biopic, *De-Lovely*, invited him to not only sing the title track for the soundtrack but to also perform the song within the movie itself.

For the first time since the Concert of Hope in 1997, there are rumours – started by Gary Barlow – that the members of Take That will perform together again before the end of the year. "We're all getting back together this Christmas for something really special," Gary, now a successful writer-producer, told *The Mirror*. "It's not strictly speaking a concert but we're doing something... and Robbie has definitely signed up to do it." Better still, his bid to break America has just acquired a powerful ally in Britney Spears; "He's hot and really sexy," she told MTV in May. "I think we should do something together and he'll blow up."

When his 30th birthday arrived on 13 February, Rob was clearly a man changed for the better. Having defied his own prophecy that he wouldn't live that long, he was instead successfully sober and grateful for his lot – years of sizable donations, hospital visits and charity work with UNICEF and his own fund, Give It Sum, had given him a perspective on his problems as he travelled the world meeting impoverished and AIDS-stricken children. He had even managed to mend one of the most important relationships in his life. As the paparazzi snapped him enjoying a quiet golfing weekend as part of his birthday celebrations at Skibo Castle in Scotland they noted that alongside Jonathan, actor-musician friend Max Beesley, ex-pat 24 star Greg Ellis and TV presenters Declan Donnelly and Ant McPartlin, Rob's dad Pete had been invited along and welcomed back into his superstar son's life.

After years of feeling ostracised, overlooked and underrated, Rob's position as the UK's most popular entertainer appears unassailable. Thanks to more than a decade's hard work, and the love and support of his family and current managers – who Jan tellingly describes as "two proud dads" – something beautiful really has come Rob's way.

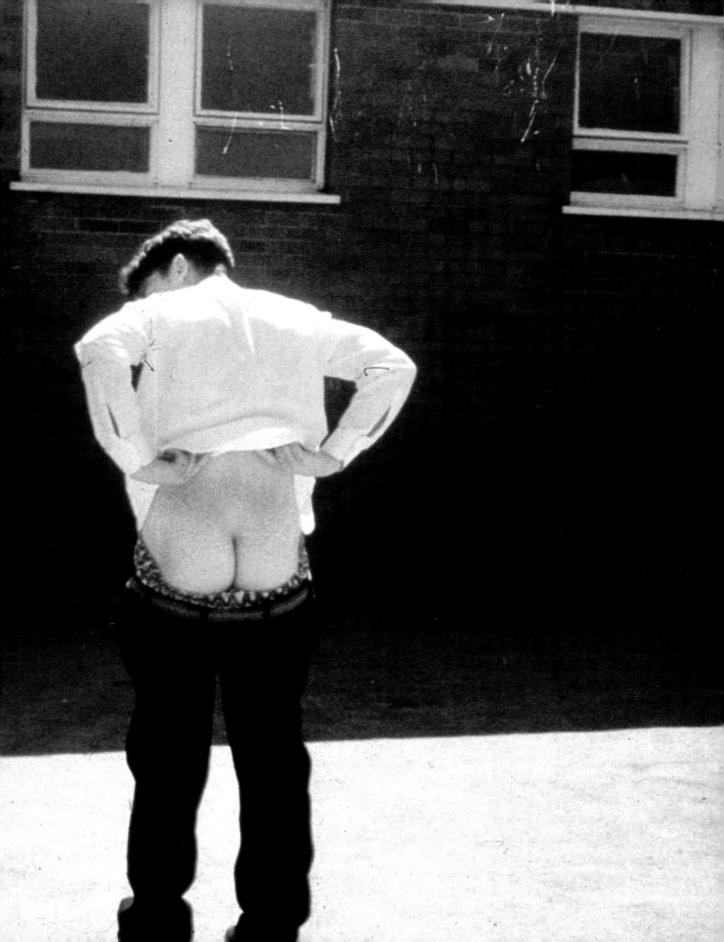